Conviction and Conflict:
Islam, Christianity and World Order

Conviction and Conflict

Islam, Christianity and World Order

MICHAEL NAZIR-ALI

continuum
LONDON • NEW YORK

Continuum

The Tower Building, 11 York Road, London SE1 7NX

80 Maiden Lane, Suite 704, New York, NY 10038

www.continuumbooks.com

First published 2006

Reprinted 2006, 2007

British Library Cataloguing-in-Publication Data
A catalogue record for this book is available from the British Library.

ISBN 0–8264–8615–0

Typeset by Kenneth Burnley, Wirral, Cheshire.
Printed and bound by MPG Books Ltd, Bodmin, Cornwall

Contents

Introduction

'Before We Begin . . .'

When I was asked to write the article on International Order for a dictionary of ethics in the 1990s, we were still struggling with the consequences of the end of the Cold War. A new international order was said to be emerging but no one quite knew what its characteristics might be. Some were loudly announcing the 'end of history', claiming that the victory of Capitalism over Marxism was final. From now on, there would be no great ideological battles on a world-wide scale, only small, regional conflicts, and gradually the assimilation of the values of capitalism by every culture and every society.[1] There were others, however, who were reminding us that most of the greater civilizations had a religious basis to them and this would bring them into conflict with one another, even if they allowed that such conflict could be ameliorated by dialogue which accepted diversity but also sought commonality.[2]

---

1   In Francis Fukuyama, 'The End of History', *The National Interest* 16 (Summer 1989) 3–18.
2   Samuel P. Huntington is, of course, the most important exponent of such ideas. See his *The Clash of Civilizations and the Remaking of World Order*, Simon & Schuster, New York, 1996.

1

There have certainly been a large number of regional conflicts, not all of them small-scale, in the last two decades or so. Some have had religion as a component, but not all. There is also a resurgence of religious ideas, movements and politics on nearly every continent. The rapid spread of Pentecostalism in Africa, Latin America and parts of Asia is already being noted by social scientists.[3] Christianity is spreading, along with other religions, in China; and in India there has been a remarkable revival of popular Hinduism. Western Europe seems to be the exception in this surge of religious belief world-wide.[4]

The most important feature of this religious ferment is undoubtedly the coming to centre-stage of Islamist resurgence. As we shall see, this has affected not only the Muslim world, but its shock-waves are being felt world-wide. A vast literature is emerging which discusses the social, spiritual, political and economic background to this phenomenon or to these related phenomena (as there may well be considerable diversity here). The organizational focus is often blurred and there is a range of ideologically-based programmes. Nevertheless, some of the characteristic ideas and inspirations are very similar.[5]

When the trustees of the Scott Holland Lectures asked

---

3 See David Martin, *Pentecostalism: The World Their Parish*, Blackwell, Oxford, 2002.

4 On this see Grace Davie, *Europe: the Exceptional Case, Parameters of Faith in the Modern World*, Darton, Longman & Todd, London, 2002; David Aikman, *Jesus in Beijing*, Regnery, Washington DC, 2003; and V. S. Naipaul, *India: A Million Mutinies Now*, Heinemann, London, 1990.

5 For a general introduction see V. S. Naipaul, *Among the Believers: An Islamic Journey*, Picador, London, 2001. For an account of developments in a particular country see Chandra Muzaffar, *Islamic Resurgence in Malaysia*, Penerbit, Petaling Jaya, 1987.

me to consider questions of theology and world order for the 2005 series, I am sure they had all of this, and more, in mind. In responding to their invitation, I decided that I would tackle the theme by considering the impact, both historical and contemporary, of Christianity and Islam on the world, as well as their relationship with one another and the huge implications this has for the present and the future. In approaching the task, it repeatedly struck me how important it was to understand the significance of the spiritual for the human condition, both as far as individuals are concerned but also for society as a whole. That is my starting point. I have then gone on to discuss the so-called 'social function' of religion in its 'cohesive' as well as its 'prophetic' aspects. This is a frank account, I hope, of the role of religion in conflict and also some comparison with other factors in conflict. In certain situations, it is necessary to see religious ideas functioning as ideology, but it is also important to recognize the role of secular ideologies in conflict.[6]

All of this brings us to the complex, painful, but also fruitful, relations between Islām, Christianity and Judaism. These are examined as they emerged, developed and mutated over the course of centuries and in different environments. Many of the issues we face today cannot be addressed without such historical understanding. The ferment in the Islamic world, which was produced as a result of the contact with modernity, is also discussed in some detail, as are the questions of culture, language and nationhood which often arose from this encounter.

---

6 See further Michael Nazir-Ali, *Citizens and Exiles: Christian Faith in a Plural World*, SPCK, London, 1998, pp. 136ff.

At the heart of these lectures, I have attempted to address matters which are central not only to Muslim–Christian dialogue, but which touch on the role of religion in plural (not necessarily pluralist) societies.[7] What are Christian, Muslim and Jewish attitudes to the state, democracy, government by consent and the possibility of dissent? This is then complemented by a discussion on the relationship between religion and law with particular reference to the Sharī'a or Islamic Law. How do eminent Muslim jurists view the matter? Is Islamic Law capable of development and, if so, how? What are the principles of movement here?

It is extremely important for world peace that there should be some agreement in the international community about the justifiability of armed conflict. What are the circumstances in which armed force may become necessary? Who has the authority to order such interventions and what is to be the form of them? Has anyone specific responsibility for reconstruction and rehabilitation after such conflict has ended? Christian traditions of Just War (but also pacifism) have traditionally provided criteria for the justifiability or not of armed conflict. Are these still relevant in a world of terrorism and counter-terrorism, of unconventional wars and of nuclear threat? Do Islamic notions of Jihād have anything to contribute to the discussion; and should Christians and Muslims be talking together about Jihād and Just War to see if any convergence is possible on when, if ever, armed conflict might be justifiable?

It is recognized that both Christianity and Islām have

---

7 For some of the issues at stake here, see Martin E. Marty, *When Faiths Collide*, Blackwell, Oxford, 2005.

questions about 'rights' based philosophies, and generally prefer to locate the individual in a context of family and community where there is a mutuality of respect and obligation which makes for the common good. Nevertheless, in a world such as ours, it is important that all sides recognize certain fundamental freedoms without which the common good itself is not served and is, indeed, damaged. There is, finally, some attention given to the relationship between terrorism and poverty. It is clear that there *is* a relationship but it is complex and varies from context to context. Who are the leaders of movements which may lead to terrorist activity, how were they formed, and who enabled them in fleshing-out and implementing their lethal agenda? What needs to be done to address the causes of this situation both in the West and in the world at large?

Each of the lectures touches on a theme which could be the subject of a book on its own. It is obvious that a single lecture cannot explore thoroughly all of the questions which are raised. I have, however, in the notes and elsewhere, tried to provide some guidance about where people may look for further information and illumination.

I am grateful to the Scott Holland Trustees for asking me to deliver these lectures in Oxford, where Henry Scott Holland was the Regius Professor of Divinity from 1910 until his death in 1918. The Trustees seek, of course, to foster the social vision of Professor Scott Holland. Throughout his life, he was concerned to relate the Gospel to the social and economic issues of human life. I hope these lectures are faithful to that vision, even if much more modest than his own projects.

I must also thank Dawn Saxton, my Personal Secretary, for assiduous attention to the preparation of the typescript; my Chaplain, Canon Christopher Stone, for various helpful suggestions; and the staff at Continuum for their assistance and their unfailing courtesy.

As always, my gratitude to my immediate family, Valerie, Shammy and Ross, for their patience and forbearance during the preparation, writing and delivery of these lectures.

> Judge eternal, throned in splendour,
> Lord of Lords and King of Kings,
> With thy living fire of judgement
> purge this realm of bitter things:
> solace all its wide dominion
> with the healing of thy wings.
>   (Henry Scott Holland)

+ Michael Roffen:
Advent, 2005

1

Rumours of Angels:
The Personal and the Social Aspects
of the Spiritual

It is commonplace these days to observe that those who make policy in our world often marginalize the role of religion. This can be the case in the area of foreign policy made by nations or multi-national alliances, it can be true of the world financial organizations, such as the World Bank or the International Monetary Fund, and it can be so with those who regulate international trade. Because religion is ignored in the initial phases of policy-making, its emergence as an important player in the lives and decisions of peoples and nations often appears as a 'surd', or irrational element, in the processes with which these organizations claim to be familiar.

It is true that some within these bodies have taken steps to ensure the greater recognition of the religious factor in national and international affairs. On the whole, however, they have been resisted from within by their colleagues, and the very nature of the organizations has had the effect of keeping all things religious at arm's length. This is shown, for example, in the President of the World Bank's initiative which attempted to use faith-communities, and their networks, in addressing holistic development and the erad-ication of poverty. From the very beginning, the project was resisted by countries like France on the grounds that it violated their avowedly secular polity; and the unit with oversight of it has no reference to religion in its title. In spite of this attempted down-grading, the project has facilitated encounter between economists, development experts and civil servants, on the one hand, and leaders of faith-communities, on the other. The former have had to recognize the extent to which these communities are already involved in the wider processes of human development and to draw them further into the mainstream of international efforts in this area.[8]

What has been attempted in international development provides important lessons for others working, for example, in the promotion of human rights, in government by consent and accountability, and in relations between nations, civilizations and blocs of one kind or another. It is refreshing, in this connection, to note some rigorous thinking being done among scholars of International Relations.[9]

The role of religion cannot be ignored, then, but what is its nature and the extent of its influence in society? Here we need to be careful of either/or answers or ones that are reductionist. The tendency in scientific description of religion, at least since the time of Durkheim, has been to emphasize the social and collective aspect of it or, to put it another way, to study symbol and ritual, with their

---

8   For an example of fresh approaches by the World Bank see the series *Voices of the Poor*, Deepa Narayan and Patti Petesch (eds): i) *Can Anyone Hear Us?* ii) *Crying Out for Change* and iii) *From Many Lands*, Oxford University Press, New York, 2000 and 2002.

9   See further Fabio Petito and Pavlos Hatzopoulos (eds), *Religion in International Relations: The Return from Exile*, Palgrave Macmillan, New York, 2003.

functions in a particular society, rather than belief and knowledge. Clifford Geertz, the anthropologist, remarks that such an approach can remain on the 'outside' of human experience, religious or otherwise. He himself prefers the *verstehen* approach of attempting to 'understand understandings not our own'. There is then the hermeneutical task of explaining to others such 'understandings' which are not their own. Of necessity such a task involves some evaluation of the systems of belief which are being studied.[10]

THE PERSONAL ASPECT OF THE SPIRITUAL

None of this is to deny the importance of the social function of religion. We shall have occasion to return to it in due course. We inhabit, however, a world where the processes of what sociologists call 'individualization' are advancing all the time. Such processes are not limited to spirituality, of course. They can include the choice of professional and leisure networks, of friends, of a spouse and of a world-view by which to live. It is vital, therefore, to consider the importance of the spiritual for the individual as well as to understand its social significance.[11]

In a sense, there is nothing new in this, except, perhaps, the extent of choice that people have. Many religious traditions have already underlined the importance of personal experience and belief. At the dawn of the modern period, the Protestant Reformers were emphasizing the experience

---

10 Clifford Geertz, *Local Knowledge: Further Essays in Interpretive Anthropology*, Basic Books, New York, 2000, pp. x, 6ff.
11 See further the Church of England report *The Search for Faith and the Witness of the Church*, Church House Publishing, London, 1996, pp. 19f., 26f.

of a saving faith as fundamental to Christian living. The pietistic movement attempted to give this an 'inward' and devotional character, drawing attention to the link between faith and being active in works of love. This concern has also been echoed in much Roman Catholic theology which has pointed to the need for actual change in the repentant sinner. The recent *Joint Declaration on the Doctrine of Justification* by the Lutheran World Federation and the Roman Catholic Church is an interesting example of how language that was thought to be in conflict has been revealed, through patient ecumenical dialogue, to be complementary.[12] For our purposes, however, the point to note is the emphasis on the person in each of these approaches. Such an emphasis was certainly true of the great Evangelical revival in the eighteenth and nineteenth centuries in Great Britain. Historians of Evangelicalism writing from very different points of view, such as David Bebbington and Callum Brown, are nevertheless agreed on the centrality of personal conversion in this movement. Whatever the differences within the movement, this remains at the heart of its self-understanding and is expressed in a variety of ways.[13]

Islām, of course, is regarded by many Muslims as a complete way of life and is characterized by elaborate codes of law (or *fiqh*) which attempt to interpret and to codify the Divine Law (or Sharī'a) in such a way as to provide guidance for the believing community even in the minutiae of its corporate life. If praying, fasting and giving are regarded as pre-eminently personal (even private) matters

---

12   Eerdmans, Grand Rapids, MI, 2000.
13   D. W. Bebbington, *Evangelicalism in Modern Britain*, Unwin, London, 1989, pp. 4ff; and C. G. Brown, *The Death of Christian Britain*, Routledge, London, 2001, pp. 35ff.

by many Christians, in Islām they have a decidedly communal (and, therefore, public) feel about them. In such a 'closed system' is there any room for the emphasis on the personal which we have noted in Christianity? The answer to this question is, of course, yes, and the tradition in Islām which focuses the importance of the person is *Tasawwuf* or, as it is more popularly known, Sūfism. It is recognized, more and more, that the roots of Sūfism, or Islamic mysticism, are in the experience of the Prophet of Islām as shown, for instance, in some of the earliest Sūras of the Qur'ān and, indeed, in those parts of the Qur'ān which speak of God's love for believers, and of theirs for him (e.g. 5:57). I have noted elsewhere that verses like the famous 'light-verse' in the Qur'ān also reveal a fine mystical sense (24:35):

> God is the light of the heavens and the earth
> The parable of his light is as if there was a niche
>   and within it a lamp:
> The lamp enclosed in glass, the glass as it were a
>   brilliant star:
> Lit from a blessed tree, an olive neither of the East
>   nor of the West, whose oil is luminous though fire
>   has scarcely touched it:
> Light upon light!
> God does guide whom he will to his light!

It has sometimes been thought that the imagery being used in this remarkable verse is that of a tabernacle lamp in a Christian sanctuary![14]

---

14 See further M. Nazir-Ali, *Islam: A Christian Perspective*, Paternoster, Exeter, 1983, pp. 60ff; and 'Love and Law in Christianity and Islam' in *A Faithful Presence: Essays for Kenneth Cragg*, D. Thomas and C. Amos (eds), Melisende, London, 2003, pp. 319ff.

Without, in any way, denying its Qur'ānic and prophetic origins, students of Sūfism have also sought other explanations for its sudden emergence at about the time of the rise of the Abbaside Caliphate. 'Allāma Muhammad Iqbāl, the great poet-philosopher of the East, and regarded as the chief advocate for the creation of the state of Pakistan, lists six reasons for the emergence of Sūfism on to the stage of history: the *political unrest* during the eighth and ninth centuries AD, which drove people of devotion to seek a contemplative life away from such conflict; the *barrenness* of much rationalistic theology which led people to appeal to a super-intellectual source of knowledge; the dead-hand of *legalism* in the major traditions and their bitter opposition to creative thinking; *inter-faith dialogue* which had been encouraged, and, indeed, practised by some of the Caliphs; and *moral laxity*, which had been brought about by unparalleled prosperity. Christians will see immediately that many of the reasons given by Iqbāl are not dissimilar to the conditions prevailing in the Eastern Roman Empire at the time of the rise of Christian monasticism in the deserts of Egypt and Syria. In this connection, it is intriguing that the final reason given by Iqbāl for the emergence of Sūfism is 'the *presence of Christianity* as a working ideal of life'. It was, however, as he says, the actual life of the monks, rather than their religious ideas, which fascinated the earliest Sūfis.[15]

Whatever the origins of this great movement within the household of Islām, and whatever the social and political significance of its great orders or *tarīqas*, it is, in the end, characterized by the personal experience of the disciple, whether that is understood in terms of what is received by

---

15 M. Iqbāl, *The Development of Metaphysics in Persia*, Bazm Iqbāl, Lahore, 1954, pp. 77ff.

grace (the *ahwāl*, states of mystic consciousness) or in the effort made by the disciple (the *maqāmāt*, stations on the journey). The conversion of Al-Ghazzāli, Islam's equivalent to St Thomas Aquinas, illustrates well the Sūfī insistence on 'conversion' or personal experience: he was a professor in the prestigious Nizāmiyya Madrassa in Baghdad when he was suddenly seized with a great fear of God during a lecture he was giving. He was unable to continue teaching and, by some accounts, lost his power of speech for a time. He resigned his position and wandered in the desert. After visiting Syria, the Holy Land and Egypt he returned to his native Tus and took up the life of a Sūfī master or *Shaikh*. From now on, his writings were concerned with living the faith through the experimental method of Sūfism.[16]

Hinduism, similarly, while it can be described in terms of the great philosophical systems it has produced or, by contrast, in the imagery of temple ritual, has one of its most ancient and most vital characteristics as the tradition of *bhakti mārga* or 'way of devotion'. *Bhakti* has always emphasized personal devotion to one or other forms of the divine: whether it is Vishnu and his important incarnations (or *avatārs*), Rama and Krishna, or Shiva and his consorts. Because of devotion to a particular god, it has tended to evolve towards henotheism and, from there, to monotheism. *Bhakti* lays stress on grace and on the love of God. For these reasons, its interaction with both Sūfism and with Christianity has been particularly fruitful. With Sūfism, it has given rise to Sikhism which incorporates both Sūfī and Hindu devotion within its sacred book, the *Guru Granth Sahib*. *Bhakti* has taken the specific aspect of Buddha-veneration in

---

16   Anne Marie Schimmel, *Mystical Dimensions of Islam*, University of North Carolina Press, Chapel Hill, NC, 1975, pp. 92ff.

most forms of Buddhism, although the extent of the veneration differs from one tradition to another. Christian interaction with *bhakti* has also produced a considerable literature and has influenced Christian hymnody and worship in most parts of India.[17]

We see then that the importance of personal experience is recognized in many religious traditions, and also that it is significant in the so-called post-modern cultural *milieu* which is becoming global. What can be said about such experience? Is it mainly acquired from our surroundings? Is it an echo from humanity's past which should not be encouraged in the future, or is it something which is innate in human beings and will continue to recur, in different forms, whatever the cultural or socio-economic context may be?

John Bowker has trenchantly criticized the idea of the 'meme' (an analogy with the gene) as a transmitter of cultural beliefs and values. This requires an essential something-or-other regarding particular beliefs which is passed on from brain to brain. Bowker points out that cultural ideas are woven from many different strands; they are not isolated 'essences' which can be passed from brain to brain without being affected by the context of social intercourse of which they are part. Professor Richard Dawkins' well-known claim that 'God is a virus' depends, of course, on meme-theory. The 'God-meme' is a meme which carries false information, rather than true, and must, therefore, be harmful to individuals as well as to society. Again, as Bowker points out, to isolate a 'God-meme' which is

---

17   Geoffrey Parrinder, *An Introduction to Asian Religions*, SPCK, London, 1958, pp. 48ff; Elizabeth Harris, *What Buddhists Believe*, Oneworld, Oxford, 1998, pp. 25ff; S. J. Samartha, *The Hindu Response to the Unbound Christ*, Christian Literature Society, Madras, 1974, pp. 128ff.

transmitted from person to person is even harder to imagine without reference to the broad cultural, religious and intellectual tradition in which it finds its meaning. For such a meme to be regarded as a parasitical 'virus' for the body politic is to read the evidence in a highly prejudiced way. Such a reading focuses on the 'harmful' or 'deceptive' aspects of religious belief, without taking adequate account of its beneficial effects.[18]

The transmission of spiritual beliefs and values is highly complex and related, in various ways, to other aspects of the human person and of the community. The processes of criticism, of distillation and of transformation are also part of the transmission in this case and, in due course, we shall have the opportunity to discuss some of these processes. What is worth saying immediately, though, is that while these great social processes roll on, more and more research is discovering that the capacity for spiritual awareness is innate in human beings, even if its expression depends on certain cultural and religious traditions. The latter can, of course, be subjected to inquiry regarding their origins, course of transmission, and the effects they have had on history as well as on the contemporary situation. This would still leave the former as a reality, on which the whole of the religious enterprise ultimately depends, and which deserves investigation on its own terms.

In fact, since the pioneering work of the Alister Hardy Institute, this is what social scientists of various kinds have been doing. In this country, David Hay and Rebecca Nye, working on the spirituality of children, have shown how the spiritual experiences of children are often *sui generis* and unformed by adults – until grown-ups either put them down

---

18   John Bowker, *Is God a Virus?*, SPCK, London, 1995, pp. 68ff.

or seek to reinterpret them in their own terms. The psychia-trist, Robert Coles, has similarly studied the spiritual experiences of children from a psychological point of view. While the experiences have often been formed in the tradition to which a child belongs, there is, according to him, a fundamental capacity and need for the spiritual to make sense of life from the early years of childhood.[19]

Looking at the matter from another perspective, the research carried out by the Alister Hardy Institute over a period of time, and involving a cross-section of the popu-lation, has shown that a least one-third of the adult population of Great Britain (often regarded as a highly sec-ularized country) are prepared to admit to a stranger that they have, at some time in their lives, been aware of a powerful spiritual experience which they have mostly understood in religious terms. It is also true to say that, in a culture which discourages conversation about religion (and politics) at social gatherings, this experience remains unart-iculated, unsocialized and intensely private. David Hay has continued with this work, along with another collaborator, Kate Hunt, in the project entitled *Understanding the Spiritu-ality of People who Don't Go to Church*. Once again, they have discovered spiritual experience to be 'a necessary part of our human make-up' and 'hard-wired' into us; but they have also seen how inarticulate people are about such an important aspect of our lives. Incidentally, it appears that people were more willing to share their experiences with Hay and Hunt because they were professional researchers from the University of Nottingham and were not seen as

---

19   David Hay and Rebecca Nye, *The Spirit of the Child*, HarperCollins, London, 1998; and Robert Coles, *The Spiritual Life of Children*, Mifflin, Boston, MA, 1990.

proselytizers. There can often be great (and sometimes unjustified) bitterness towards formal religion alongside considerable spiritual awareness.[20] It is interesting, in this connection, to note that the World Health Organisation's continuing multi-faith and multicultural project on spirituality and human well-being has also uncovered a similar sub-stratum of spiritual awareness in a wide cross-section of cultures and contexts.

Whether it is publicly expressed or privately held, socialized and maturing or fitful and perhaps stunted, personal spiritual experience enables people, to a greater or lesser extent, to make sense of their lives and of the world around them. It often provides a framework of living in the present and direction for the future. It helps them to love and be loved, to have hope and to see meaning in the ordinary. Any account of the role of religion in our world must take due account of such personal belief and experience.

THE SOCIAL ASPECT OF THE SPIRITUAL

However, whatever we may say about the importance of religious belief for the individual, there is no doubting its significance for society. Any careful student of history will be aware of the role of religion in social cohesion, through the provision of an overall spiritual and moral framework for particular societies and also through the power of symbol and ritual to provide *foci* for communal solidarity.

---

20 See further *The Search for Faith*, p. 4; D. Hay and K. Hunt, *Understanding the Spirituality of People Who Don't Go to Church*, University of Nottingham, 2000. For a historical background to spiritual experience see William James' classic *The Varieties of Religious Experience*, Penguin, New York, 1982.

Sociologists of religion since Emile Durkheim have tended to take a 'functionalist' approach to religion. By this they have meant that religion serves certain social purposes which may not be immediately obvious from its belief-system or ritual. They call these the latent functions of religion. Such functions allow societies to recognize themselves as such, to provide for the assertion and reassertion of social solidarity, and to be one of the means for social control by invoking a transcendent moral order from which flow rules of behaviour. Religion offers a world-view within which people's commitments are reinforced, their conflicts justified, their suffering valued and their ultimate questions, both personal and social, answered.

So far, so good; such a description does justice to one aspect of religion which believers would recognize. What then is the problem? It lies, I think, in the further claim made by some sociologists that the 'latent functions' of religion have been, or are being, taken over by other agencies, whether that is the state, voluntary organizations or, indeed, professional and leisure networks. Modern society can, according to them, increasingly deliver on the conditions for human welfare, and democracy provides all the legitimation it needs. There is no necessity for an appeal to a higher order of being.[21] In this connection, it is interesting to learn that the work of those sociologists who have a committed religious perspective, such as those who worked under the label *sociologie religieuse*, is often dismissed as 'unscientific'. Why? Because they were interested in how religion continued to shape society and because they

---

21   See, for instance, Bryan Wilson's account in *Religion in Sociological Perspective*, Oxford University Press, Oxford, 1982, pp. 32ff.

refused to be relativistic in the assumptions they brought to their work.

Wilson states, at the very beginning of his now almost classic work that sociology is a 'product of western civilization'. Such a statement may be open to challenge on a number of fronts. From our point of view, however, we have to note a complete absence of discussion of the work of Ibn Khaldūn (1332–1406), the great North African social historian, who is often regarded as the father of modern sociology. Is this because Western scholars are unable to conceive of a Muslim scholar, writing in the fourteenth century, who could, as Professor Akbar Ahmed points out, 'write in terms of cause and effect, of drawing universal conclusions on the basis of observable phenomena, and one who could discuss the movement of societies in terms of social dynamics and not as a direct consequence of God's will'.[22] For all his 'scientific objectivity', however, Ibn Khaldūn, as Akbar Ahmed notes, remains a believer. His interpretation of *'asabīyyah*, or social cohesion, is based on a spiritual view of the world and of human society. Human beings are God's representatives on earth (Q2:30), and human social organization must reflect this trusteeship.[23] In more ways than one, Ibn Khaldūn resembles the Christian practitioners of religious sociology, labelled 'unscientific' by those who claim to adopt a 'value-free' approach but whose values are, in fact, undeclared.

The so-called effectiveness of the modern state is mostly limited to the delivery of material benefits. The rules of

---

22   Wilson, *Religion in Sociological Perspective*, p. v; Akbar Ahmed, *Islam under Siege*, Polity, Cambridge, 2003, pp. 74ff. See also Akbar Ahmed, 'Ibn Khaldūn's Understanding of Civilisation' in the *Middle East Journal* 56, 1 (Winter 2002), pp. 1ff.

23   Ahmed, 'Ibn Khaldūn's Understanding of Civilisation', p. 77.

public engagement are such as to be devoid of any commitment beyond the formal – and where they do invoke
transcendental ideas, such as the dignity of the human
person, they are drawing on the reservoir of past Christian
values based on the faith of the Church. How long can a
nation continue to live on the reserves of its spiritual
tradition? While sociologists may describe the *effectiveness*
of contemporary government, they do not tell us the precise
areas in which it is effective. Without spiritual values
informing its policies, can it really be effective in safeguard-
ing that view of human dignity which is not simply
utilitarian; the stability of marriage and the family, so
deeply rooted in religious tradition; in preventing the
misuse of drugs and alcohol; and in promoting the selfless-
ness of service to the community and even sacrifice for the
nation? The content, then, of the modern state, held as an
ideal by these sociologists, is limited to the provision of
economic need and a rights-based philosophy which often
militates against the common good.

Already in the 1960s, Peter Berger, the Austro-American
sociologist, who had been a disciple of Max Weber, was
beginning to see the futility of a 'value-free' approach. It
tended towards an implicit atheism and to marginalize
religion in the modern world. At first he tried to modify his
method, and then abandoned it, seeking to replace it with
a social study of religion drawing on explicitly theological
perspectives. He has identified 'signals of transcendence'
which are to be found in any human situation. There is, for
example, the fundamental human propensity towards *order*,
and the corresponding fear of disorder. Such a propensity,
and such a fear, have usually been explained in religious
terms by holding that order in human society reflects an
underlying order in the cosmos itself – the divine order that

supports all human attempts at ordering. It is not that all (or any) of these attempts are perfect or even justifiable. It is rather the *instinct* for order which is itself remarkable. The 'explanation' that it is built into us to ensure the survival of the species is not complete in itself, as the question can be asked *why* that should be so, if the universe shows no signs of order but is, rather, random and disordered.

The Bible's rejection of a cyclical view of the human condition, its insistence on a linear view of time which makes the future significant and worth fighting for and waiting for, is perhaps its most significant legacy to the contemporary world. Without the biblical view of time there would be little room for *hope*, another of Berger's 'signals of transcendence'. Whether our eschatology is religious or purely secular, we are inevitably oriented towards the future. This is in terms both of our personal expectations and of the group's well-being and development. Berger mentions other 'signals of transcendence' and these include the human sense of justice (as well as outrage at manifest injustice), the significance of art, music and sport, and the existence of humour.[24]

In *After Virtue*, Alasdair MacIntyre sketches out the kind of moral and spiritual amnesia which so-called 'value-neutral' approaches to history and sociology have brought about. The canons of these disciplines will allow their practitioners to chart the succession of one spirituality and one morality after another; but they will prevent them from

---

24   Peter L. Berger, *A Rumour of Angels: Modern Society and the Rediscovery of the Supernatural*, Penguin, Baltimore, MD, 1969. His later book, *The Heretical Imperative*, Collins, London, 1980, explores the applicability of an inductive approach to religious experience.

relating which tend towards greater personal and social order and which towards disorder, which for authentic human flourishing and which for self-indulgence. This alleged 'value-free' paradigm of social science supplies the resources for a spiritual and cultural relativism which refuses to affirm what is beneficial in a particular tradition or to disapprove of dispositions and behaviours which damage the social fabric of a nation. In such a context, MacIntyre urges the construction of new forms of moral and spiritual community in the context of which virtue-based living is possible. Nor is this simply a counsel of despair: he points to the way in which the arrival of monasticism from the East gave people like St Benedict a form of living together which, on the one hand, refused to identify with a decadent social order and, on the other, was able to resist the encroaching barbarism.[25]

Much is being said these days, and rightly, about 'Mission-Shaped Church'.[26] In a highly mobile and rapidly changing society it is extremely important for the Christian presence to be expressed in ways which are accessible to the cultures in which it finds itself. The authenticity of each expression will, indeed, need to be judged in the light of what the Bible and the Great Tradition have to say about the nature of the Church and the varying ways in which its life can be expressed.[27] In terms of MacIntyre's programme, however, we also need to ask whether churches, in whatever way they are structured, can be moral and spiritual

---

25 Alasdair MacIntyre, *After Virtue: A Study in Moral Theory*, Duckworth, London, 2nd edn, 1985, pp. 4ff, 263.

26 See further the Church of England report, *Mission-Shaped Church*, Church House Publishing, London, 2004.

27 Michael Nazir-Ali, *Shapes of the Church to Come*, Kingsway, Eastbourne, 2001, pp. 71ff.

communities which, on the one hand, are able to see through the ruling paradigms of the cultures in which they find themselves and, on the other, can be islands where the divinely-given virtues of faith, hope and love are transforming individuals in such a way that they can withstand the approaching darkness of spiritual and moral anarchy. Such communities will then truly show the world what difference the good news of the arrival of God's Kingdom, in the Person of Jesus, can make to individuals, families and nations. As Lesslie Newbigin has said, they will be an effective 'hermeneutic of the Gospel'.[28]

In *The Death of Christian Britain*, Callum Brown has placed the issue of Church decline squarely within the abandoning of the nation's core religious and moral identity. From being a faith which undergirded every aspect of national life, and provided people with a moral code by which they could live, as well as spiritual succour in times of difficulty or failure, Christianity has rapidly been consigned to the margins of national life. Its moral and spiritual vision is no longer the means by which individuals, families and communities order their lives.[29] Such ordering as there is left is now based on highly privatized notions of not causing harm to others (understood in a utilitarian and individualized sense) and on various nostrums of self-fulfilment which abound in the media and in the libraries. In this context, Professor Oliver O'Donovan has pointed out[30] that what will most shape the life of Christians (and churches) in the West, during this century, is the loss of

---

28   Lesslie Newbigin, *The Gospel in a Pluralist Society*, SPCK, London, 1989, pp. 222ff.
29   Brown, *The Death of Christian Britain*, pp. 2ff.
30   In a submission to the Evangelical Alliance's Commission of Inquiry on Faith and Nation, 2004.

connection between Christianity and the formative legal and political culture of the Western world.

In spite of these, what Joan Lockwood O'Donovan has called 'dissolvents', at work in various communities, it remains true that historically (and in many parts of the world, today) religion has been the basis for social cohesion. It lies at the root of most moral traditions, and many of the most enduring moral systems have been elaborated within a religious framework. It can readily be conceded that non-religious people can act morally, even altruistically, and that they may be, in some cases, morally better informed. Still, what is at issue here is whether religion can give a *better account* of the rise of moral awareness and of fundamental moral principles, such as the primacy of conscience, the equal dignity of all human beings and our sense of duty. As even Kant saw, such an account can best be given by reference to a Supreme Being who is both the ground for such ideas and the one who makes them attainable, if not in this life, then in the next.[31]

Religion, and the moral tradition of which it is often the guardian, are also related to the development of law. It is, of course, true that what is spiritually and morally desirable may not always be appropriate for legislation. There is, nevertheless, a very real connection between moral and spiritual values, on the one hand, and law, on the other. Law must have sound spiritual and moral underpinning if it is to be effective in the long run. Neither following public opinion (formed these days more and more by the mass media) nor brute coercion should be the 'drivers' for

---

31 Immanuel Kant, *Religion Within the Limits of Reason Alone*, Harper, New York, 1960, pp. 6, 131, 170ff; see also M. Nazir-Ali, 'Thinking and Acting Morally', *Crucible*, October–December 2002, pp. 207ff.

law-making, though it is recognized that, in a democracy, public opinion should be taken into account and there *is* a coercive aspect to law. Even in highly secularized contexts, two principles which most underlie legislation are those of liberty and the prevention of harm. Both have strong spiritual and moral connotations. Liberty is deeply rooted in Christian ideas of conscience and responsibility for our actions. Where the notion of 'harm' is concerned, it is far from clear that this applies only to individuals. It must also include harm to society and to those institutions which society needs for its survival and prosperity. These certainly include marriage and the family, as well as the sacredness and dignity of the human person. Thus marriage and family law must ensure that the abiding 'goods' of these institutions are not harmed and that people within them are never treated merely as a means. Hence, even in a secular dispensation, there must be a safe-guarding of monogamy and the life-long nature of marriage.

In one way or another, religion is also often related to the emergence and development of a nation's institutions, whether these be monarchy, government by consent in various forms, or various kinds of civic bodies and institutes for higher education. Even in cases where there has been an explicit separation of Church and State, as in the United States of America, the foundational documents still invoke transcendental beliefs. It may be that, in due course, the religious aspect of social institutions is eroded, in some cases to the point of becoming vestigial. It does, nevertheless, serve to remind those involved of what lies at the base: the coronation as a service of consecration, prayers in Parliament, chapels in colleges and hospitals, each in a different way tells us of the spiritual basis of our social organization. In this connection, it is interesting to note that, according to Callum Brown, nothing has replaced Christianity, as an alternative ideology, even in a rapidly secularizing situation: 'no new religion, no new credo, not even a state-sponsored secularism'.[32] The dangers of deliberately creating a spiritual and moral vacuum, by removing the remaining signs of a definite spiritual basis, will be obvious. What might fill such a vacuum in a world of competing religions and ideologies?

THE PROPHETIC ASPECT OF THE SPIRITUAL

While the cohesive aspect of religion has been important for nearly every society, in the Judaeo–Christian and Islamic traditions particularly, religion has another very important function. This is the prophetic role of a community of faith and, indeed, of individual believers. The Old Testament scholar, Walter Brueggemann, in his book *The Prophetic Imagination*, set out the prophetic task as nurturing, nourishing and evoking a consciousness and perception *alternative* to the consciousness and perception of the dominant culture. Such an alternative consciousness will critique any order which exploits and oppresses, denying people their proper freedom. It will, at the same time, *criticize* the refusal of the offer of God's newness by clinging on to the privilege of the past and present, and *energize* the community so that it can move with hope towards the future. Brueggemann sees Moses as the paradigmatic prophet who brings into being an alternative community which is based on its rejection of the false hierarchy of Egypt and is formed as a people on the basis of

---

32   Brown, *The Death of Christian Britain*, pp. 2–3.

its recognition that God has wrought a mighty deliverance in bringing it out of slavery. As with Jeremiah, the truly prophetic will grieve at the faithlessness of the existing order, and thus its coming destruction, but it will also nurture seeds of hope in a coming liberation. Just as the Cross of Jesus is the ultimate criticism of the old order of sin and death, so the Resurrection is *par excellence* the energizer towards the new future, bringing recreation and hope in the midst of destruction and despair.[33]

In Islām also, the Prophet of Islām's initial proclamation of the One God, Allah, who is just and requires justice in human society, led to a hostile response from the leaders of Mecca whose prosperity it threatened.[34] This prosperity was at least partly built on the popular pilgrimages to the city and the cult of the so-called 'daughters of Allah', Al-Lāt, Al-Manāt and Al-'Uzzā, as well as of other gods. It was also built on a particularly nasty kind of usury and on social customs which Muhammad condemned. Again and again in Muslim history, the 'prophetic' aspect of Islām has been manifested: whether in the revolt of the *Khārijites* who rejected the emergence of a hereditary and worldly caliphate, or in those Sūfīs who saw through the attempts of political and religious leaders to uphold a kind of dead orthodoxy as merely using religion to prolong a particular order. Muslim reformers in the nineteenth and twentieth centuries also criticized corruption and exploitation in their own day, and today much of the energy of resurgent Islamism arises from such a 'prophetic' view of the relation

---

33 Walter Brueggemann, *The Prophetic Imagination*, Fortress Press, Philadelphia, PA, 1978.
34 On this early period see Martin Lings, *Muhammad: His life based on the earliest sources*, Islamic Texts Society, Cambridge, 1991.

of religion to society. From our point of view, such attitudes cannot be neglected or minimized.

Even if Judaism, Christianity and Islām are traditions where a 'prophetic' aspect is emphasized, this does not mean that other traditions do not have such a side to them. Just to take a couple of examples, Sikhism emerged on the historical horizon as a result of vigorous interaction between the *bhakti* (or devotional) tradition in Hinduism and the preaching of the Sūfīs. This led to the emergence of a non-denominational devotionalism which lies at the root of the Sikh founder Guru Nānak's teaching. This teaching laid stress on monotheism and on a personal knowledge of God, but it was also characterized by a rejection of caste and the practice of social equality, symbolized by the practice of eating together.[35]

Much earlier, of course, the Buddha himself had drawn on anti-caste traditions within Hinduism and proclaimed social equality. The Buddhist teaching on the need to eliminate suffering can also bring Buddhists up against unjust and oppressive governments which cause or increase suffering. Their identification of desire as the cause of suffering leads them to resist unbridled consumerism, and their commitment to non-violence requires that they should be critical of militarism in any form.[36]

It is true, of course, that religions, as they have developed historically, do not always fulfil their prophetic vocation. There is a temptation to compromise with the powerful and the wealthy. Religious traditions can buttress the existing order without asking whether such an order is unjust. It is also the case, however, that religious traditions sometimes

---

35 *Sikhism: Way of Life*, Gurdwara, Gravesend, n.d.
36 Harris, *What Buddhists Believe*, pp. 99ff.

experience a renewal of the 'prophetic'. This may be because of the work of a charismatic individual, like Mahatma Gandhi or Martin Luther King; or it may be because of particularly difficult political and economic circumstances, as with the rise of theologies of liberation in different parts of the world. This aspect of religious belief has often empowered individuals and groups to affirm their own identity and dignity. It has given them the tools for the criticism of the social and political *milieu* which they inhabit. It has, from time to time, given the poor, even the dispossessed, tools to challenge the wealthy, and the powerless tools to challenge the powerful. It has provided people with resources to live in a prophetic way, the way of 'critical solidarity'. Here is not a love 'that asks no questions'. Indeed, it asks many questions for the sake of the common good, and may make those in authority very uncomfortable.

It is perhaps appropriate to note at this point that the rise of Islamism in so many parts of the world, to which we shall give some attention later, has at its best tried, however clumsily and even destructively, to recover the prophetic side of Islām which has sometimes been obscured by self-serving and compromised leadership. This does not, by any means, justify all the views held by the variety of organizations and individuals grouped under this label. Nor does it, in any way, condone the methods which they have employed. It is simply to recognize a very real aspect of the phenomenon.

We have seen then the importance of personal experience of the spiritual. We have also considered the ways in which religious traditions provide cohesion and direction for communities and nations. Finally, we have taken account of the 'prophetic' aspect of at least some religious traditions, which can be used to empower ordinary people so that they can make a significant contribution to the reform and the renewal of societies in which they have to live.

2

The Role of Religion in
Conflict and Peacemaking

Some people will say that the account of the role of religion
in the lives of individuals and of societies given in the last
chapter is a highly idealized one and does not correspond
with the experience of many. They will say that it is more
of an apology for religion than a critique. Is not religion the
cause of endless conflict in families, local communities,
within and between nations? How is this side of religion,
which a few might even claim is its *only* side, to be
evaluated?

It is certainly true that religious belief, and formal aspects
of religion, have sometimes been, and still are, a powerful
ingredient in many conflicts. In the West, people often
associate the so-called 'wars of religion' with a great deal of
suffering in middle Europe and, for many, the Peace of
Westphalia (1648) marks the dawn of the modern age, at
least in political terms. The principle of non-interference
on religious grounds was established and people were recognized as citizens regardless of religious affiliation.[37] The
succeeding 'privatization' of religion was to ensure that

---

37 See Owen Chadwick, *The Reformation*, Penguin, London, 1990, pp.
318ff, 444ff.

religion should not again be a major element in conflict between nations. It is, however, a simplification to reduce the causes of conflict in Europe during the early modern period simply to religion. There were many other factors involved, including political intrigue, the national interests of France, Sweden, England and Holland, as well as factors such as state envy of ecclesiastical property.

To consider another period, whilst the origins of the crusades are complex, the obstructions caused for pilgrims to the Holy Land by the Seljuk Turks and the perilous state of the Eastern Christians were two main reasons why they were undertaken. A third might have the desire of Pope Urban II to encourage the knights and soldiers of Western Europe to engage with the Turks and the Arabs in the East rather than fight one another.[38] Whatever the reasons for the crusades being undertaken, the crusaders, from time to time, behaved like barbarians and with great brutality, ruthlessly exploiting and oppressing local populations. It has to be remembered that the crusades were never solely directed against Muslims, Turks or Arabs, but against Christian Byzantium itself, against the Jews and the Albigensians, and there was even a demand that the Holy Roman Empire's wars with Protestants should be declared a crusade! The Lebanese writer Amin Maalouf has distilled from contemporary Arab chroniclers the Muslim Arab view of the crusades. Like the Christian accounts, it is, of course, biased; but it does establish that the Eastern Christians suffered at the hands of the crusaders, that some of the crusading armies were barbaric in the treatment of those they conquered, and that the overall effect of the crusades

---

38   Steven Runciman, *A History of the Crusades* (Vol. I), Penguin, London, 1991.

was to weaken the position of the Eastern Christians.[39] Once again, we find that religion is a significant factor on both sides, but there are many others: both the Turkish and the European desire for land, for example, the need to secure peace in Europe by diverting attention to the situation further away or the need to secure Western Europe from further Muslim invasion.

Examples of religion as an ingredient in conflict are not limited to interaction between Christians and Muslims. In both the Hindu epics, the *Mahābhārata* (of which the *Bhagavadgita* is part) and the *Rāmāyana*, religion is used to justify participation in conflict. The Emperor Ashoka, until his conversion to Buddhism, was engaged in wars of conquest; and even Buddhism could not prevent such wars of conquest and succession in the kingdoms of South-East Asia. In fact, in some cases, it was involved in the course of the conflicts and their consequences.[40] The policies of the Mughal Emperor Aurangzeb were designed to roll back the tolerant regimes of his forebears and to turn the Mughal Empire into a Muslim state with the strict enforcement of Sharī'a, or Islamic Law, as he understood it. He ordered all newly-built Hindu temples to be torn down, the traditional poll-tax or *jizya* was revived, and various campaigns were undertaken against 'infidel' areas. One of these, against the Sikhs, resulted in the capture and execution of the ninth Guru, Tegh Bahadur, causing enduring bitterness among the

---

39   Amin Maalouf, *The Crusades Through Arab Eyes*, Al-Saqi Books, London, 1984.
40   For details of such conflicts see Keith Taylor, 'The Early Kingdoms'; Kenneth Hall, 'The Economic History of South-East Asia'; and J. G. De Caspario and I. W. Mabbett, 'Religion and Popular Beliefs of South-East Asia Before c.1500' in *The Cambridge History of South-East Asia* (Vol. I), Cambridge University Press, Cambridge, 1994, p. 157f.

Sikhs. Aurangzeb's policies were responsible for turning the Sikhs into a militarily effective body which could combat Mughal oppression.[41]

Wittingly or unwittingly, British imperial policies, such as the introduction and extension of separate electorates in India, led to the strengthening of communal identity, of which religion was a significant marker. Each socio-religious community developed its own political organization and this became a base for religious nationalism. The Muslim form of it was expressed, of course, in the demand for Pakistan, and the Sikh form in the struggle for Khalsastan or a land for the Sikhs. It is the Hindu form, however, which has caused a huge setback to the Congress brand of secularism which guarantees the freedom and equality of all citizens regardless of religious belief without marginalizing the influence of religion in the public sphere.[42]

Religious movements, such as the *Arya Samāj*, provided the background to overtly communal movements like the *Shiv Sena* and the RSS (Rashtriya Swayamsevak Sangh) and these, in turn, have spawned political movements of the BJP (Bharatiya Janata Party) sort! 'Indian-ness' is now being identified with being 'Hindu' and the other communities, Muslims, Christians, Sikhs, are having their loyalty to 'Mother India' questioned if they do not agree, at least culturally, to be Hindus.

In *India: a Million Mutinies Now*, the well-known expatriate Indian novelist, V. S. Naipaul, describes both the populism of the *Shiv Sena* and its politics based on fear of

---

41   John Richards, *The Mughal Empire*, 1995, in *The New Cambridge History of India*, CUP, Cambridge, 1988– , pp. 171ff.

42   Kenneth Jones, *Socio-Religious Reform Movements in British India*, 1997, in *The New Cambridge History of India*, CUP, Cambridge, 1988– , pp. 218ff.

the 'other', whether Muslim, Christian or Dalit. Alienation is a common theme and each group is afraid that it might be extinguished by the others. Naturally, in such an atmosphere, communalism flourishes and Gandhian (but also Christ-like) non-violence is despised. An officer of the *Shiv Sena* is quoted as saying: 'I have contempt for Gandhi. He believed in turning the other cheek. I believe that if someone slaps you, you must have the power to ask him why he slapped you, or you must slap him back. I hate the idea of non-violence.'[43]

This mix of religion with communal and nationalistic chauvinism may be somewhat surprising in post-Gandhian India, but is not limited to it. At the height of the Civil War in Bosnia, I had occasion to visit the region on behalf of Christian Aid. We met with people from each of the communities and it was interesting to discover how closely ethnicity and religion were identified. This was particularly so with the Muslims who seemed ethnically and culturally very similar to the other Serbs and Croats *except* for their religious affiliation (which, in many cases, simply extended to their name and a dim memory of ancestors). In the Bosnian context, however, the identification of Serb nationhood with being Orthodox was clearly to the fore and, to a great extent, drove the 'ethnic cleansing' of Muslims from Serb areas and beyond. In a similar way, the situation in Kosova is characterized by one community (the majority) being Muslim and the other, the Serbs, being Orthodox Christians. Our aim had been to cooperate with Islamic Relief and other organizations so that humanitarian aid could be delivered on a non-confessional basis. In the event, this proved difficult because the communities were,

---

43   Naipaul, *India* (as note 4), p. 24.

by then, so radically polarized.[44] A more recent visit to the region has only reinforced my impression that ethnicity and religion are still very significant for the conflict there.

The identification of ethnicity and nationhood with a particular religious tradition is also characteristic of post-Soviet Russia where the Orthodox Church is seen as central to the meaning of being Russian. This raises questions about the place of other religious communities, such as Jews, Muslims and Buddhists, as well as other Christian Churches, in that country. These questions remain unsettled to date and, indeed, are growing sharper with the passage of time.[45]

Many other examples of religion being an ingredient in ethnic or nationalist conflict can be given: Northern Ireland, for instance, shows us that there are significant political and social factors in the situation there; but it cannot be denied that hopes and fears about the religious future of the various communities are a real aspect of the conflict.

RELIGION CAN GO WRONG

We have to admit frankly that, for good reasons and bad, religion has contributed and continues to contribute to conflict of various kinds and at different levels. We can agree, moreover, that religion can and does go wrong. If, as we have seen, religious or spiritual awareness is innate in us,

---

44 For an account of the conflict see Laura Silber and Allan Little, *The Death of Yugoslavia*, Penguin/BBC, London, 1995.
45 James Billington, *Russia: In Search of Itself*, Woodrow Wilson Center, Washington, DC, 2004.

then, like other fundamentals of our existence, it will be possible for this to go wrong in a variety of ways, both personal and social. Just to take another example, love is a basic human experience: to give it and to receive it makes us more fully what we have been created to be. Love has many facets to it and we can have parental love or filial love, the love between man and woman, the love of friends and, of course, our love of God. In every one of these manifestations love can go wrong. It can become demanding, cloying, and jealous, or turn in on itself, so that we selfishly seek our own fulfilment rather than seeing love as giving to the other.

Patriotism, or love of country, is greatly to be admired. We are social beings and, as the Russians put it, we need *sobornost* or togetherness in a number of ways. One of these is being part of a people or nation. Such a sense of solidarity makes for the common good, provided it is not turned in on itself, becomes excluding and exclusive, or promotes xenophobia and suspicion of the 'other'. We have seen already how any and all of these can happen, jeopardizing regional and world peace.

Just as love and patriotism can go horribly wrong, so can religion. A properly biblical anthropology should alert us to this possibility. The Reformers' emphasis on the 'total depravity' of human nature does not mean that every aspect of our nature is utterly corrupt but that everything about us, our minds and reason, our hearts and emotions, our impulses and desires have all been touched by that fundamental rebellion of ours which is properly called sin. Even the good we wish to do is affected by this underlying and overarching reality, and religion is not excepted from it.

COOPERATION AND COLLABORATION
IN PEACEMAKING

It would be a mistake, however, to capitulate entirely to the somewhat fashionable view that not only nature but human society as well is 'red in tooth and claw' everywhere; to accept conflict, in other words, as our paradigm for interpreting the world around us. As a matter of fact, both the natural world and human society are characterized as much by cooperation as by conflict. Scientists are beginning, more and more, to see the importance of symbiosis in driving forward the engine of evolution and, indeed, in the day-to-day life of flora and fauna.[46] In his opening address to the 1988 Lambeth Conference, Robert Runcie, then Archbishop of Canterbury, spoke of cooperation and interdependence between humanity and the rest of creation as the 'Creator's plan'. Throughout history human societies have developed internal structures, such as the division of labour, which allow different sections to contribute to the overall good. It is true that such structures have been exploited and distorted by those with power, so that workers have not been given what is justly due to them or have suffered discrimination because of the nature of their work. No one has, however, doubted the need for structures of cooperation if social, economic and political life is to be possible. Similarly, peoples and nations, while often engaged in conflict among themselves, are also capable of cooperating for reasons of trade, pilgrimage or regional peace. Religious belief is sometimes an impulse towards

---

46   See further Ursula Goodenough, *The Sacred Depths of Nature*, Oxford University Press, New York, 1998, pp. 83ff; and Michael Behe, *Darwin's Black Box: The Biochemical Challenge to Evolution*, Simon and Schuster, New York, 1996, pp. 188ff.

cooperation, and religious organizations, both formal and voluntary, can provide the means for dialogue and peace-making in a number of different ways.

During my visit to Bosnia, at the height of the conflict there, I came across small Christian groups already engaged in ministries of reconciliation and peacemaking. They were, it seemed, sowing their seed in most unpromising soil; often people knew *exactly* who had killed their relatives or friends. It was nasty, dangerous work and yet these groups were engaged in it largely because of their beliefs.

In an important contribution to a debate in the House of Lords on the role of religion in promoting international order, the then Archbishop of Canterbury, George Carey, pointed out that international diplomatic and government circles are sometimes reluctant to allow people of faith to play a part in peacemaking. When, however, they are permitted to do so, their role can be quite significant. He told the story of how the civil war in Mozambique was brought to an end by the efforts of Dinis Sengulane, the Anglican bishop there, and the Roman Catholic lay community of Sant' Egidio, based in Rome.[47] George Carey was also instrumental in initiating the dialogue among Jewish, Christian and Muslim leaders on peace in the Holy Land which led to the historic Alexandria Declaration. The Rabbis for Peace movement seeks to ensure justice, repara-tion and compassion for the *Palestinian* people and there are significant groups of Shī'a 'Ulemā (or Islamic 'Clerics') in countries like Iran who seek the way of dialogue.

Such dialogue is almost indispensable for world peace today and can be simply about people of different faiths

---

47   Speech on 15 October 1999. See also Andrea Riccardi, *Sant' Egidio: Rome and the World*, St Pauls, London, 1996, especially Ch. 3.

sharing *information* with one another regarding their respective beliefs so that misunderstandings may be removed. It can also be about the sharing of experience, so that each is led to describe what is at the core of their commitment. Sometimes it happens that people are alerted to their own situation in a particular way: they recognize that there is tension between different groups which needs to be defused, instances of injustice against a particular ethnic or religious community which need to be addressed, or an agreed programme in the building up of community which needs to be developed. In each of these cases, *common values* have to be identified for the sake of joint action, and often this can only come about through dialogue between people of different faiths. Dialogue is also becoming more and more important as a vehicle for different faith traditions affirming *fundamental human rights and responsibilities*, in the light of each tradition and wherever a particular tradition has influence. We shall have an opportunity to consider this in more detail when we discuss the issue of reciprocity.[48]

There is a need for dialogue about peace in many different situations. In this country, Christians have often been at the forefront in engaging people of other faiths in dialogue, particularly on questions of harmony in the community, access to services, and racial justice among a host of other matters. In places like India there is a need for dialogue on the precise place of Hinduism in Indian society and the freedom which followers of other faiths can expect to worship, to live according to the tenets of their faith, and to be able to share their faith with others. In a very similar way in the context of

---

48 See further M. Nazir-Ali, *Mission and Dialogue: Proclaiming the Gospel Afresh in Every Age*, SPCK, London, 1995, pp. 75ff; and Nazir-Ali, *Citizens and Exiles* (as note 6), pp. 115ff.

Sri Lanka, the place of Buddhism has to be properly understood and how the freedoms of others are upheld.

THE ABRAHAMIC FAITHS AND PEACE

The term 'Abrahamic' can be problematic because each of the faiths which understands itself in this way has a somewhat different view of Abraham: the Jewish people, naturally, regard him as their primal ancestor, the Christians as their spiritual forebear in *faith*, and the Muslims as their ancestor through the line of Ishmael as well as the archetypal Muslim. Even if problematic, however, 'Abrahamic' is a convenient label for all three faiths and we have to consider their situation with regard to peace in the world.

Judaism has had an enormous influence on the world in which we live. Some of this, undoubtedly, has been through Christianity and Islām but some has been direct. In the ancient world, both in the Roman Empire and well beyond that, the Jews were present as significant communities. One estimate is that they formed a fifth of the population of the Eastern Roman Empire, and it is certain that there were Jewish communities as far afield as The Gulf and even South India.[49] Such estimates of population and distribution raise questions about the nature and extent of Jewish mission, and on this score there is a vast literature. It is clear that an important aspect of this mission was *apologetic*: that is, it had to do with explaining what the Jewish people believed to those among whom they lived. This was, sometimes, literally a life and death matter for Jewish

---

49 See John Stambaugh and David Balch, *The Social World of the First Christians*, SPCK, London, 1986, pp. 46ff.

communities in the diaspora. It seems also to be the case that at least some Jews wanted to influence the morals of the Gentile world. Even without admitting explicitly proselytizing activity, many scholars concede that an educational, moral and apologetic mission had the effect of gathering a large number of God-fearers to the fringes of synagogues in Gentile cities, and a smaller number of proselytes, or formal converts to Judaism, were also joined to these communities. The pages of the New Testament tell us how this strong Jewish presence in the ancient world was both an obstacle and a preparation for the Christian mission. Carleton Paget has shown, however, that Jewish mission cannot simply be limited to the apologetic, moral and educational but that there was, from time to time and from place to place, a proselytic dimension to this mission which serves as an important background to the otherwise sudden irruption of the Christian mission in the first century AD.[50]

Except for some communities (such as the Jews of different parts of India), the Jewish people in the Middle Ages lived under the domination of either Islamic rule in the Middle East, or of European Christendom. They were, however, able not only to survive but to make a notable contribution to each civilization. Under Islām, Jewish scholars often wrote in Arabic. Moses Maimonides is acknowledged as a philosopher of the first rank. He attempted a synthesis of Judaism and Aristotle which has many points of contact with the syntheses being attempted by other scholastics, Muslim and Christian. He wrote in both Hebrew and Arabic and was a noted presence at the

---

50 See further Carleton Paget, 'Jewish Proselytism at the Time of Christian Origins', *Journal for the Study of the New Testament* 62 (1996), pp. 65ff.

Caliph's court. Ibn Kammūna wrote an *Examination of the Three Faiths*, a work which can be regarded as perhaps the earliest exercise in the comparative study of religions. In Europe, Jewry was much more concerned with the strengthening of its inner life than with wider interaction with culture. The Jews made a singular contribution, however, as a bridge between the world of Islām and the West: in the main they were the vehicle for transmitting back to Europe the riches of Greek philosophy, science and ethics which had been translated into Arabic, often with the help of oriental Christians, and then studied, commented upon and improved by the Muslims.[51]

Today also the Jewish people continue to be influential, not least in leading people and nations to reflect on the Holocaust in which millions of Jews were imprisoned, tortured and murdered. On the one hand, the Holocaust reminds us of other instances of genocide, such as the Armenian or the Assyrian, and, on the other it raises profound questions for theology. George Steiner, in his autobiography, is only too aware of the sufferings of the Jewish people throughout history and asks whether even the most sublime mission makes them justifiable. He cannot, however, get away from what he calls 'the indispensable miracle of Israel'. He means not the modern nation-state 'armed to the teeth', but the nomadic tribes which have survived determined attempts to exterminate them by nations and civilizations much greater than them. However difficult the vocation, does it point to a providential origin?[52]

Since the Second World War, there has been much

---

51 Nazir-Ali, *Islam* (as note 14), pp. 23, 71 and *passim*.
52 George Steiner, *Errata: An Examined Life*, Weidenfeld and Nicolson, London, 1997, pp. 48ff, 158ff.

dialogue between Jews and Christians. Much of this has focused on addressing the alleged anti-Semitism of Christian history in Europe. Many Jews and Christians regard the roots of the Holocaust as lying in these attitudes, even if they were given a 'pagan' twist by the Nazis. The dialogues have been concerned to promote mutual understanding and to remove conscious and unconscious prejudice. There have been especial attempts to ensure that the public reading of the New Testament and liturgical worship do not, in any way, encourage attitudes of rejection towards the Jewish people.[53]

THE FAITH, THE LAND AND JUSTICE

There does, however, remain a thorny issue which is not adequately addressed and that is the question of the land.

Continual cycles of conquest and capitulation, nomadic incursion and settlement, invasion from sea and from land, have given the land we call holy a decidedly mixed history and, with it, a mixed population. Throughout the ancient world, and even today, people of different faiths and ethnic origins invest the land in which they live with a greater or lesser amount of sacredness. The origins of Israel then, whether these are understood in terms of intruding semi-nomads or of the further organization of peoples already in Palestine, or of both, have to be understood in the light of this plural background. Similarly, Israel's understanding of the land which was to be theirs has to be understood in the

---

53 See further Helga Croner (ed.), *Stepping Stones to Further Jewish–Christian Relations* and *More Stepping Stones to Jewish–Christian Relations*, Stimulus, London, 1977, 1985.

context of 'belonging to a place', which is so common. Even the biblical accounts in the books of Joshua and Judges of the unification of land and peoples leaves us in little doubt as to the mixed population of the time, and this situation seems to have continued well into the monarchical period.[54]

Consciousness that the land was theirs by divine promise was widespread in early Israel. This theme dominates the Bible and is used hundreds of times in a variety of ways. The gift of the land was, however, *conditional*. It required certain kinds of moral and cultic behaviour and without these God's covenant with his people could be broken and they could lose the right to continue living in the land (Deut. 4:25–27; 1 Kgs 9:6–7; 2 Kgs 17:5–15, 18; Jer. 9:13–16). Indeed, Jeremiah thought that the covenant was so completely broken that a new one was needed in its place (Jer. 31:31). In spite of their dire warnings to a fickle and rebellious people, however, the prophets seem to continue hoping against hope that Israel would repent and that God would restore the land to his people (Jer. 16:14–15; Ezek. 36:8–15). It has been noted that part of the 'conditionality' which attaches to the land has to do with Israel's treatment of the stranger or alien in its midst. The stranger was not to be oppressed and was to be treated as a native (Lev. 19:33–34). Wages were not to be withheld from strangers and the poor generally (Deut. 24:14) and justice was to be meted out impartially (Exod. 12:49; Deut. 1:16, 24:17, 27:19).

---

54 See further M. H. Woudstra, *The Book of Joshua*, Eerdmans, Grand Rapids, MI, 1981, pp. 9ff; A. D. H. Mayes, *Judges*, Sheffield Academic Press, 1985, pp. 66ff; Naim Ateek, *Justice and only Justice: A Palestinian Theology of Liberation*, Orbis, New York, 1989, pp. 103ff; Gerald McDermott, *Evangelicals and Israel*, Ethics and Public Policy Center, Washington, DC, November 2003, pp. 8–9.

From the time of the Exodus, a 'mixed multitude' went with the Israelites and even during the conquest they concluded various kinds of agreement for co-existence with different groups of people (Exod. 12:38, Josh. 9, Judg. 1:16, 19, 21, etc.). All of this suggests, first, that there is ample precedent in the Bible for us to recognize the possibility of peaceful co-existence between Israel and other people in the land. This is true of the very narratives which speak of Israelite conquest and it seems to have been true throughout the biblical period. Ezekiel's vision of re-settlement after the Exile includes a portion for the strangers who reside with Israel (Ezek. 47:21–23). Secondly, and perhaps more importantly, the Bible shows us the centrality of *justice* in Israel's dealings with the people roundabout. There can be no enduring peace without such an understanding of biblical and theological justice.[55]

THE HOLY CITY IN THE HOLY LAND

What can be said of the land as a whole can also be said of Jerusalem, its main city and capital of many kingdoms. In its pre-Israelite days it seems to have been a stronghold of the Jebusites. While its conquest is reported in Joshua (10:1, 22–27) and in Judges (1:8), it seems clear also that Israel *could not* (Josh. 15:63) or *did not* (Judg. 1:21) drive out the original inhabitants and seems to have co-existed with them until well after the rise of the monarchy (2 Sam. 24:15–25).

---

55 This is the burden of Naim Ateek's *Justice and only Justice*, especially Chs 4 and 8.

The first reference in the Bible to Jerusalem appears to be in the story about Abraham (still called Abram) and the priest-king Melchizedek, King of Salem (usually taken to be Jerusalem; the encounter itself takes place in a valley near Jerusalem). This is a most remarkable passage (Gen. 14:17–20): a Canaanite priest-king (the very thing Israel was told to destroy) brings Abraham, the father of the faithful, bread and wine, and blesses him. Abraham then makes him an offering. What are we to make of this incident? Many of the historical details lying behind the story have been confirmed by recent archaeological and literary discoveries. Von Rad comments that, 'Melchizedek, in his veneration of God Most High, maker of heaven and earth, came close to believing in the one God of the world, whom Israel alone knew . . . Such a positive, tolerant evaluation of a Canaanite cult outside Israel is unparalleled in the Old Testament.'[56] However, it is not only an evaluation of a cult that is at stake here. Melchizedek is later taken as a justification for the sacral kingship of the Davidic king: thou art a priest for ever according to the order of Melchizedek (Ps. 110:4). Our Lord himself refers to this Psalm in a messianic context (Mk 12:35–37 and parallels) and, certainly, later Christian reflection relates the priesthood of Melchizedek to the eternal and unchanging priesthood of Christ himself (Heb. 6:20–7:25).

From the time of the Exile onwards, Jerusalem has been ruled by the Babylonians, the Persians, the Greeks and the Romans. The last named destroyed it in AD 70 as a reprisal for a rebellion, and then in AD 135, after suppressing another revolt, re-founded it as a pagan city, *Aelia Capitolina*, which the Jews were forbidden to enter. A Gentile-led church

---

56   Gerhard von Rad, *Genesis*, SCM Press, London, 1972, p. 80.

continued to survive there until the conversion of Constantine when, because of the influence of his mother, Helena, it began to become the important site of pilgrimage it is today. The See of Jerusalem, which was suffragan to Caesarea, was raised to patriarchal dignity at the Council of Chalcedon (AD 451). From the time of St Cyril (304–386) onwards, Palestine, and particularly Jerusalem, began to be seen as 'the fifth Gospel', an important place not only of pilgrimage but of residence for pious Christians, even though the New Testament, conscious of the Church's universal mission, lays little stress on the land as such, whether for Jews or for Christians.[57]

Jerusalem's capitulation to the Muslims in AD 638 brought yet another religious tradition to the Holy City. Muslims regard the land and the city as holy apparently because it is so called in the Qur'ān (5:23) and because the Prophet of Islām is said to have performed the *mi'rāj*, or his journey to heaven, from the Temple Mount (cf. Q17:1). It is for this reason that the Caliph 'Abd Al-Malik built the Dome of the Rock there in AD 691 to rival the Christian pilgrimage site of the Holy Sepulchre. The Al-Aqsā mosque is nearby. Whether or not the site mentioned in the Qur'ān is the one presently identified as the place of the Prophet's ascension – and there is much debate on this issue – it has certainly acquired this sense in Muslim piety and there are many incentives to visit it and to worship in it.[58] It is also true, of course, that the siting of the third holiest shrine of Islām (after the *Ka'aba* in Mecca and the Prophet's Mosque in Medīna) on the Temple Mount itself poses almost

---

57 Ateek, *Justice and Only Justice*, pp. 113ff.
58 See further Colin Chapman, *Whose Promised Land?*, Lion, Oxford, rev. edn, 2002, pp. 289ff.

insoluble questions as far as the future of Jerusalem is concerned.

The point of this potted history is, of course, to show that Jerusalem has been settled, invaded, destroyed and resettled by people from many different ethnic and religious backgrounds. Both Christians and Muslims have, for centuries, regarded the city as holy to them and have important sacred sites there. Any settlement would have to take this into account. In Jewish prophecy the City has often been presented as a place for all nations: it is where they gather (Isa. 2:2–4; Mic. 4:1–4), where the Lord provides a feast for *all* peoples (Isa. 25:6–8), and where the temple becomes a house of prayer for all (Isa. 56:7 cf. Mk 11:17).

The Jewish people make a strong claim to both land and city. It is where their ancestors arrived in the course of their nomadic journeys. It is a land which they conquered and settled; where their judges and kings ruled until the great disruptions of the eighth and sixth centuries BC, and to which, after much waiting and longing, they returned from Exile. It is from here that they were scattered, once again, in the reign of Hadrian (AD 135), and to which they have desired ardently to return, especially in the prayer, 'Next Year in Jerusalem'.

Even here, however, there are complicating factors: biblical Israel cannot be identified *simpliciter* with Rabbinic Israel as reconstituted after the Synod of Jamnia (c. 100 AD). As I have said before, there is evidence that Judaism was an actively missionary faith in the ancient world and claimed a substantial number of formal adherents as well as a considerable and influential fringe. It seems clear also that there were conversions in Eastern Europe and elsewhere at a later date. How 'Jewish' are the *Falasha* of Ethiopia or the *Bani Israil* of Bombay? A significant number of recent immigrants to the State of Israel are thought to be Gentiles taking the chance to get out of Russia or Ethiopia, so much so that there were reported to be 'judaizing' centres for their reception and integration. It is possible still for anyone to be instructed for a period by an orthodox Rabbi, to convert, and thus to acquire the 'right to return' to Israel.[59] Understandably, Ateek asks whether Palestinian Arabs are not more entitled to the land than these very late arrivals.

But if the question, 'Who is a Jew?' is a problematic one, so is the question, 'Who is an Arab?' Even during the Prophet of Islām's lifetime there were notable Jewish tribes in Arabia. When Islām expanded, after his death, into the rest of the Middle East, North Africa and south-western Europe, the Christian, Jewish and other peoples of the region gradually became 'Arabicized'; Arabic first became a *lingua franca* between conquered and conqueror, and eventually became the main language of society, even if the religious and ethnic communities sometimes clung on tenaciously to their scriptural and religious languages. The process of 'arabicization' is complex and difficult enough to assess in its earliest manifestations, but it was accompanied by a mainly political process more recently which attempted to integrate various Christian communities into the Arab nation. This was resisted by the oriental Jews because Zionism was already in the air and their eyes were set on Palestine. Their history of both glory and tragedy cannot be ignored.[60] As we have seen, from the beginning

---

59   See further Stambaugh and Balch, *The Social World of the First Christians*, pp. 41ff; Ateek, *Justice and Only Justice*, p. 105; Arthur Koestler, *The Thirteenth Tribe*, Random House, New York, 1976.

60   Kenneth Cragg, *The Arab Christian*, Mowbray, London, 1992, pp. 52ff; and Bat Ye'or, *The Decline of Eastern Christianity under Islam*, Associated University Presses, New Jersey, 1996, pp. 200ff.

Palestine has seen a great mobility of populations and this is no less true of the modern period. Ye'or claims that European Muslims from the Balkans were settled in Palestine in the nineteenth century, as were people from the Caucasus and Central Asia. Chapman also admits that it was first the Crusades and then the Zionist enterprise which alerted Muslims to the significance of the land for them.[61]

However, it remains true that whatever we may say from the point of view of history, the Jewish people, wherever they may be and however long they have been there, invariably have a strong attachment to the land and the city. They want access to it, to visit it, to worship there and, if possible, to live there. This sense of belonging is based on strong ethnic, cultural, historical and religious factors. It must be taken into account in any thinking about the land.

In the same way, the Palestinians are there in the land. This is 'a fact on the ground' which no one has been able to deny. Many of the Christian and Muslim communities make ancient claims about their presence in the land, and it is clear that the presence of most of them predates the beginnings of Zionist settlement in the land.

Here then are two peoples claiming the same piece of territory and the religious aspects of the claim are very much to the fore. Whatever the Christian (and even Jewish) background to a spiritual understanding of the promised land, this will not wash with millions of Jews who have left their homes from India to Morocco and from Moscow to New York to live in *Eretz Israel*. Christian and

---

61 Bat Ye'or, *The Dhimmi*, Associated University Presses, New Jersey, 1985, pp. 385ff; and Chapman, *Whose Promised Land?*, p. 297; see also McDermott, *Evangelicals and Israel*, p. 12.

Muslim Palestinians, similarly, understand at least part of their *raison d'être* to be custody of their respective holy places. Neither side will be driven out by the other and those who have proposed it on either side are living in a world of fantasy. A way has to be found for these people to live in the same land and the same city. Unfortunately for us, a *one-state* solution, which might have been possible *if* the British had sought to fulfil *all* of the aspirations expressed in the Balfour Declaration, never saw the light of day. Later on, the Palestine Liberation Organisation (PLO) aspired to a unitary state where at least some Jews and non-Jews could live together. Hamās and Islamic Jihād also struggle for a unified state which would be Islamic in character and where Jews and Christians would have to live in accordance with the Sharī'a. Such a charter clearly causes deep and widespread concern.

Since 1988, however, the PLO has accepted a two-state solution with Israel and Palestine living side by side and, more or less, in peace. This is now also the official position of the Government of Israel and of the international community. Once again, though, there are several intractable problems. The return of Palestinian refugees is one of them: how many can return to their homes, now mostly within Israel? Is financial compensation acceptable for those who cannot return? Who will pay? Israel alone or the international community as well? There is then the very real issue of Jewish settlements in the West Bank. Will secure access to them by Israel turn any Palestinian state into a number of *de facto* Bantustans, ensuring Israeli hegemony? There are other issues, such as the sharing of scarce resources like water. But the most dramatic of them is easily the future of Jerusalem.

The UN plan for the partitioning of Palestine (1947)

envisioned Jerusalem and the area surrounding it as an 'international zone'. This kind of thinking was also supported by many countries and churches and, indeed, accepted by Israel! It is recognized now, however, that both Palestinians and Israelis feel the need for sovereignty in Jerusalem so strongly that they are unwilling to give it up, even to the international community.[62] Internationalization, therefore, as a possible solution has given way to some kind of shared sovereignty. Israel has continued to claim sovereignty over the whole of Jerusalem, but it is said that Prime Minister Barak, at the 2000 Camp David talks, *did* offer Palestinians some sovereignty over parts of Jerusalem. It is thought that the negotiations broke down over the question of control of the Holy Places.

The Anglican position on Jerusalem, as reflected in the Lambeth Conference 1998 Resolution V.20, is similar to the stance taken by the Eighth Assembly of the World Council of Churches meeting in Harare only a few months later. It urges an open and inclusive city, with access for people of all faiths and shared sovereignty between Israelis and Palestinians. The Harare Assembly refers to a Joint Memorandum by the Patriarchs and Heads of Christian Communities in Jerusalem, which calls for the application of a special statute for the protection of Holy Places in Jerusalem, which are to be regarded not simply as monuments but as living centres of community life.[63] Both

---

62   Colin Chapman, *Whose Holy City? Jerusalem and the Israeli–Palestinian Conflict*, Lion, Oxford, 2004, p. 183.

63   *The Official Report of the Lambeth Conference 1998*, Morehouse, Harrisburg, PA, 1999, pp. 427ff; *Together on the Way, Official Report of the Eighth Assembly of the WCC*, Diane Kessler (ed.), World Council of Churches, Geneva, 1999, pp. 187ff; Chapman, *Whose Holy City?*, pp. 244ff.

the Roman Catholic Church and the Church of England have also drawn attention to the importance of international law in the governance of relationships between Israel and the Palestinians.[64]

With so many layers to the problem and with such volatility, it is difficult even to hazard a guess at what might work. It is perhaps enough to note that the trend in recent negotiations seems to be inching towards Palestinian sovereignty of at least some parts of the city and Israeli sovereignty over others, with overall municipal cooperation. The question of the settlements remains, as does the complexity of the Old City and the Holy Places. It is possible to imagine a formula for shared sovereignty covering the latter with actual governance by an interreligious council and with freedom of access to all guaranteed by the international community. As Colin Chapman has well said, 'If we will it, it is not a dream'.

TWO FAITHS WITH A MISSION

Jewish influence affects nearly every aspect of human learning, culture and policy. It is, however, Christians and Muslims who have propagated, far and wide, the original monotheistic vision of Israel. This can be seen in the provision of an intellectual basis for the unity and order of the universe or in the idea of time as being genuinely open, epigenetic, as James Ward would have said,[65] leading to a

---

64 Chapman, *Whose Holy City?*, p. 202; R. Harries, *After the Evil*, OUP, Oxford, 2003, p. 150.
65 See further James Ward, *The Realm of Ends*, CUP, Cambridge, 1912, pp. 97ff.

view of the world that is *both* evolutionary and teleological, or in securing the basis for the unity of humankind. Each has modified the vision for its own purposes. Christians have emphasized the story of the Creation and the Fall, for example, in developing an understanding of the human situation. They have found the moral and spiritual world of the written prophets more compelling than, say, much of the ritual and ceremonial material in the Pentateuch, though they have recognized the importance of the moral teaching there in, for instance, the Decalogue. Naturally, they have seen all of it pointing to and being fulfilled in Jesus of Nazareth and in the universal mission of the Church following his death and resurrection.[66]

In many ways, Islām is much more at home with the ritual and ceremonial world of the older Testament but also with its prophetic aspect, even if it does not acknowledge any need for direct access to the prophetic corpus of Israel. The biblical prophets, along with others, and their message, as understood in the Qur'ān, are regularly mentioned and venerated. Fasting and feasting, praying and pilgrimages, rules about living and loving, war and peace all find their analogues in the story of Israel.[67]

In the course of their development, both Christianity and Islām have been deeply influenced by the different cultures which they have contacted, notably the different varieties and layers of Hellenism in the ancient world. This has been hugely creative for both traditions, but also problematic in that it has tended to obscure the semitic foundation of each.

---

66   F. F. Bruce, *This is That*, Paternoster, Exeter, 1968.
67   See A. Geiger, *Judaism and Islam*, Madras, 1898.

This is perhaps more true of certain forms of Christianity than it is of Islām.[68]

It is, of course, the 'missionary' nature of these two faiths which has enabled them to universalize the knowledge of the God first revealed to Israel. By the term 'missionary' I mean the commitment, throughout history and in the mainstream of both faiths, to seek a response from people of every kind to their message. The word itself does not occur in the fundamental texts of either. For Christians the basic idea is that of 'sending' (*apostellein* and related expressions in Mk 6:7; Matt. 10:5; Lk. 9:2, 10:1; cf. Jn 20:20), though 'welcoming' in the ministry of Jesus and of the apostolic Church is also important. In Islām it is 'invitation' or 'calling' which is basic (*da'wah*). This may be understood as a calling to Islām, or submission to God, as in the preaching of the Prophet of Islām, or as a call which reminds people of their original state in which they were created as Muslims, or those who had submitted to God, and to which they are invited to return. In this sense, Islām is, *par excellence*, the natural religion (or *dīn al-fitra*).

However the 'missionary' vocation is understood, it is clear that these two are now *the* missionary faiths in the global arena. This raises the spectre of conflict between

---

68 Where Christianity is concerned, there is a vast literature but see, for example, C. K. Barrett, *The New Testament Background: Selected Documents*, SPCK, London, 1961, especially pp. 54ff; R. D. Sider, *The Gospel and its Proclamation: Message of the Fathers of the Church*, Michael Glazier, Wilmington, DE, 1983, pp. 60ff; J. N. D. Kelly, *Early Christian Doctrines*, A&C Black, London, 1985, pp. 11ff; but see also N. T. Wright on the limits of pagan influence in *The Resurrection of the Son of God*, SPCK, London, 2003, pp. 33ff. For Islam see R. Walzer, *Greek into Arabic*, OUP, Oxford, 1962; and De Lacey O'Leary, *How Greek Science Passed to the Arabs*, London, 1949; M. Nazir-Ali, *Frontiers in Muslim-Christian Encounter*, Regnum, Oxford, 1987, pp. 15ff; and Nazir-Ali, *Islam*, pp. 70ff.

them when they compete with one another on the same territory. In fact, such conflict has already begun to occur in places like northern and central Nigeria and in eastern Indonesia. If such conflict is to be prevented, it is important, first of all, for each faith to acknowledge the missionary character of the other. This in itself defuses some of the tension. When I was Bishop of Raiwind in Pakistan, the town from which the See took its name was well-known as a railway junction but for little else – *except* that it was the international centre for an Islamic missionary movement known as the *Tablīghī Jamā'a* (or the organization for the Propagation of Islamic Teaching). We had reasonably good relations because each side recognized the missionary nature of the other. Once this happens, conversation and co-operation about what is good for the community can take place at a number of levels. In an ever more tense situation, Archbishop Josiah Idowu-Fearon of Kaduna in northern Nigeria has promoted dialogue with Muslims without any sense of compromise on either side. Such a dialogue has to do with increasing understanding of what is important to each side in matters of faith and practice, and also with peacemaking and peacekeeping in the local situation. There have been many serious ups and downs in this relationship but, as far as I know, the dialogue has never completely been derailed. During a recent visit there, I was privileged to meet many of those who are part of this bridge-building programme.

In a rapidly globalizing context, all kinds of institutions and organizations are accountable at the bar of world opinion. This is especially so where the prevention of conflict is a leading concern, and where the justifiability of embarking on armed conflict of any kind has to be demonstrated. Religions are particularly exposed to such accountability, and Islām and Christianity, in particular, have to bear the burden of much expectation. Not only are they deemed to be accountable to international opinion but there is also *mutual accountability*; religious people can no longer claim the luxury of sorting out problems having to do with the freedom of minorities, the position of women in society, the use of violence to further political, social or religious aims, and many others, on a purely 'internal basis'. The whole world is interested, and particularly people from other faiths in dialogue with those of the faith concerned.

In one way or another, Christianity and Islām represent well over half of all the people in the world and that proportion is increasing. The rest of the world has a proper interest in how their relationship with one another is managed. Fortunately for us, the history of their interaction provides many lessons, both positive and negative, as to the future. In this case, it is certainly true that we must learn from the past for the sake of the present and the future. It is to this rich and varied history of relationships that we now turn.

3

Encounters and Clashes: Muslims, Christians and Jews from the Beginning

As we have seen, Muslims affirm that Islām is the original or 'natural' religion of humans (*dīn al-fitra*). It was the religion of Adam (and of Eve) before they erred and it has been the religion of each of the prophets. In this sense, what is said of Abraham in the Qur'ān is also true of all the prophets (3:67).[69] Whatever one may make of this claim, it is certain that Islām in its historical, cultic and legal forms has its origins in the intense spiritual experience of Muhammad, the Prophet of Islām. It was this experience which changed him as a person and it was this experience which underlies his religious, as well as his social and political programme.[70]

Such an understanding of the origins of Islām shows us also that there has never been a time when Muslims have not been in contact with Christians and Jews. The earliest accounts of awareness and of recognition that Muhammad had a prophetic mission invariably involve Christians. The

---

69 See, for example, John Esposito, *Islam: The Straight Path*, Oxford University Press, New York, 1988, pp. 20ff.

70 Fazlur Rahmān, *Islam*, Weidenfeld and Nicolson, London, 1966, pp. 13ff.

Christian monk, variously named Bahīrā or Nestūr, who recognized the signs of prophethood on him when he was still young, and Waraqa bin Naufal, cousin of Khadīja, the Prophet of Islām's first wife, who confirmed that he was the expected Arabian prophet, are just pointers to a ubiquitous Christian presence in and around the Arabia of the time.[71] Jews, similarly, are supposed to have anticipated the coming of this prophet, and the list of Jewish tribes with whom the Prophet concluded the Constitution of Medīna amply testifies to the major presence the Jews were on the Arabian Peninsula.[72]

When Muhammad began his preaching of a strict and exclusive monotheism, he was naturally opposed by the leaders and residents of Mecca who felt that their cult of the daughters of Allah, Al-Lāt, Al-Manāt, and Al-'Uzza, which had established their city as a place of Pan-Arab pilgrimage, was threatened. Not only did they oppose him and seek to do him harm, but also his followers, so much so that Muhammad had to consider the possibility of refuge for them. He was protected by his uncle Abū Tālib, but they were unprotected and at the mercy of their tormentors. He decided that they should migrate to the Empire of Abyssinia which included, at that time, parts of the region of Yemen. This is described in Muslim tradition as the first *hijra* or migration.[73] In this connection, it is interesting that the Prophet chose a Christian country for the refugees; a

---

71 Ibn Ishāq, *Sīrat Rasūl Allāh*, trans. A. Guillaume as *The Life of Muhammad*, Oxford University Press, Karachi, 1987, pp. 79ff; Philip Hitti, *History of the Arabs*, Macmillan, London, 1970, p. 111; and William Muir, *The Life of Mohammad*, Grant, Edinburgh, 1923, p. 21.

72 Ibn Ishāq, *The Life of Muhammad*, pp. 90ff, 231ff.

73 Ibn Ishāq, *The Life of Muhammad*, pp. 117ff; Hitti, *History of the Arabs*, pp. 113ff.

country, moreover, which he described as one of justice and righteousness. The refugees were greeted hospitably and passed their time in peace and comfort. Even if the complete agreement between them and the Negus reported by Muslim traditionalists is regarded as a somewhat romantic reporting of history, there seems to have been enough serious theological dialogue to justify at least some of the convergence reported between the two sides.[74]

When the Prophet of Islām had acquired a number of followers in the town of Yathrib (which the Jews called Medīna and which came to be called Medīnat Un-Nabī – the town of the Prophet), he sent more of his followers there. Eventually, he escaped from Mecca himself and arrived in Medīna. This is the second or the great *Hijra* with which the Muslim calendar commences. Almost as soon as he had arrived, he promulgated a historic document known variously as the Constitution or Covenant of Medīna. Here a single umma or community is created which includes refugees from Mecca and their hosts in Medīna, Muslims, Jews and even unbelievers, all bound together in terms of a solemn social contract, under the terms of which all are treated equally. The situation was extremely volatile, however, and the cordial relations with the Jews did not last long. The contract did not, therefore, endure but, for its time, it is a most remarkable document and ought to have greater influence in the development of Islamic polity than it does. Today, there are many projects for an Islamic State in different parts of the world. The question is: would such a state be modelled on the Constitution of Medīna; and if not, why not?

---

74 Muir, *The Life of Mohammad*, pp. 68ff; and Ibn Ishāq, *The Life of Muhammad*, pp. 146ff.

Although relations with the Jews of Medīna deteriorated rapidly, partly because of the Muslim perception that they were a fifth column in their midst, treaties with Jews elsewhere were still possible, even if they were concluded after bloody battles. The treaty with the Jews of Khaibar allowed them to continue tilling the land on condition that they pay a tribute of half the produce.[75]

We have noted already the cordiality which existed between the Muslim refugees in Abyssinia and their hosts. Relations with the Christians of Najrān too were amicable. As in Abyssinia they were based on previous theological discussion: after some preliminary discussion about the nature of God and the Holy Trinity, the Christians asked the Muslims whether 'Isā Ibn Maryam (Jesus the Son of Mary) was the Son of God. When the Muslims denied this (what else could they do, having denied that Allah could have daughters) the Christians played their trump card asking, 'But who then is his father?' The Qur'ān seems to have two different responses to this question. It consistently calls Jesus the Son of Mary, thus reversing the usual Semitic tendency to use patronymics and investing a term used dishonourably in Jewish-Christian polemic with honour. The other is a counter-question: 'Whose son was Adam?' or 'Who is Adam's father?' The answer to this in the Qur'ān is that he was created by God's creative command, '*kun fa-yakūnū*' (be and it is – 3:59) just as Jesus was in Mary's womb (4:171, 19:35).

It is worth noting that these Christians were not only accommodated in the Prophet's mosque at Medīna, but that the Prophet allowed them to offer liturgical prayer there.

---

75 Ibn Ishāq, *The Life of Muhammad*, pp. 510ff; Muir, *The Life of Mohammad*, pp. 375ff.

Medīna (along with Mecca) is now one of the two shrines from which non-Muslims are excluded on pain of death.[76] Although, once again, there was not complete theological agreement, there was enough to conclude a treaty, which in some ways was to serve as a model for the ones which were soon to come. It may be worth risking a generalization and saying that relations, in those early days, were better with Christians than with Jews.

THE GLOBAL EXPANSION OF ISLAM

When the Prophet died in AD 634 there was a serious rebellion among the various tribes of the Peninsula who had pledged loyalty (*baiʿa*) to Muhammad, but on his death regarded themselves absolved from their oath. For the first of the righteous Caliphs, Abū Bakr, the main task during his brief reign was to regain Arabia. This he did through the work of the able general Khālid bin Walīd, *Saif Allah* or the sword of God. His methods were so severe that the second Caliph ʿUmar relieved him of his command. As Philip Hitti puts it, 'Arabia had to conquer itself before it could conquer the world.'[77]

The martial tribes of Arabia, now no longer spending their time feuding among themselves, needed an outlet for their zeal and enthusiasm in their new found faith. Very quickly we find them spilling over into the Fertile Crescent, following up, as it were, Muhammad's letters to the rulers round about Arabia.[78] One by one, the great cities of the

76 Ibn Ishāq, *The Life of Muhammad*, pp. 270f.
77 Hitti, *History of the Arabs*, p. 142.
78 On these letters see Ibn Ishāq, *The Life of Muhammad*, pp. 652ff.

Christian Middle East surrendered to the Muslims. Hitti regards this rapid spread of the Muslims as of a piece with the periodic movements of Semitic people from the desert to more settled lands (the movement and the organization of the Hebrews as a people in the Promised Land also being an example of this kind of change in the demography of the region).[79]

In AD 635, abandoned by the Byzantine garrison, Damascus capitulated peacefully, its gates being opened by the family Al-Mansūr, the family of the one who was to be the great St John of Damascus. The gates of Jerusalem were opened for the Caliph 'Umar by the Patriarch Sophronius who escorted him into the city and invited him to pray in the Church of the Holy Sepulchre. 'Umar is said to have refused on the grounds that if he did so, the Muslims might use it as an excuse to turn the Church into a mosque. He is supposed to have prayed outside and, true enough, Muslims later built on the site a mosque known as the Mosque of 'Umar.[80] Alexandria was more difficult to subdue and it took two attempts by the Muslims, as well as treachery on the part of the ecclesiastical authorities, for it to fall. Within twenty years or less of the Prophet's death, the mainly Christian lands of Syria (including Palestine), Egypt, Mesopotamia and even parts of North Africa were in Muslim hands. Nor was this the end of the matter: the Persian Empire was wholly conquered and Byzantium lost its fairest provinces, but more was to come with Muslim advances into Spain and southern France, on the one hand, and the lands around the Indus on the other. It was only in the centenary year of the Prophet's death that the Muslim advance in the West was checked

---

79 Hitti, *History of the Arabs*, pp. 10ff.
80 Nazir-Ali, *Islam* (as note 14), p. 37.

when Charles Martel stopped the Muslim armies between Tours and Poitiers.

One consequence of such movements of people is the displacement and dispersal of others. At the time of the Caliph 'Umar it was decided, on the basis of a prophetic tradition, that Arabia should have only one religion and the Jewish and Christian communities, long settled, were sent into exile. The remaining Jews of the Khaibar fled to Palestine to the environs of Jericho, and the Christians of Najrān to Syria and Iraq. As we have seen, during the Prophet's lifetime at least some Jews and Christians had continued living in Peninsular Arabia.[81] During the period of the conquest other communities were similarly displaced and dispersed. There were also communities that were destroyed in the course of the campaigns both within and outside Arabia.[82] To preserve the racial and martial purity of the Arabs a system of discrimination also developed between Arab and non-Arab. The conquering Arabs lived in military cantonments (rather as the imperial British were to do centuries later) and the native populations were left to their professions and the cultivation of the land. Even when they converted to Islām their status was different from that of the conquerors. Gradually, this state of affairs was ameliorated by the *mawālī* system, whereby a non-Arab Muslim could affiliate with an Arab tribe. Eventually, of course, the rising tide of the arabicizing *mawālī* overtook the people from the desert and assimilated them into the cultures that were emerging.[83]

---

81 Hitti, *History of the Arabs*, p. 169.
82 Hitti, *History of the Arabs*, pp. 1140ff; Ye'or, *The Dhimmi* (as note 61), pp. 140ff; and Nazir-Ali, *Islam*, pp. 30ff.
83 Hitti, *History of the Arabs*, pp. 169ff; cf. *The Cambridge History of Islam*, P. M. Holt *et al.* (eds), CUP, Cambridge, 1977, pp. 65f.

THE EMERGENCE OF THE *DHIMMA*

From all of this ferment emerged the *dhimma*. The word means responsibility or protection and implies that Muslim rulers have a responsibility to protect their non-Muslim subjects. Its seeds lie in the treaties which the Prophet of Islām had himself concluded with the Christians and Jews, and it is based on a verse of the Qur'ān, 'Fight those who do not believe in Allah or the Last Day and who do not observe the due prohibitions prescribed by Allah and his Apostle and who do not acknowledge the True Religion from amongst the People of the Book until they pay the *jizya* (or poll-tax) submissively and acknowledge their insignificance' (9:29). Historically, the provisions of the *dhimma* were first articulated at the time of the capitulation of the major Christian cities: Damascus, Jerusalem and Alexandria. At this time, the inhabitants were simply guaranteed their security on payment of the *jizya*. Later, when agricultural land was involved, this was extended to include the *kharāj* or land-tax which, in some cases, had to be paid even after conversion to Islām.[84]

Although the *dhimma* was, at first, limited to Jews and Christians, it was later extended to Zoroastrians and even further than that. The *Chachnāmeh*, for instance, a history of the Arab conquest of the Sind by Muhammad bin Qāsim (c. AD 711), tells us that the conditions of the *dhimma*, including the *jizya*, were imposed on Hindus and Buddhists.[85]

---

84 Hitti, *History of the Arabs*, pp. 171, 218f; Ye'or, *The Dhimmi*, pp. 165ff.
85 Hitti, *History of the Arabs*, pp. 168f; 'Alī Kūfī, *The Chachnāmeh* (trans. Mirza Kalichbeg), Vanguard, Lahore, 1985, pp. 164ff.

As the terms of the *dhimma* evolved, it tended to become more and more restrictive. The so-called ordinance of 'Umar, which is ascribed to the second Caliph but was probably fully developed at the time of the puritanically inclined 'Umar bin 'Abd Al-'Aziz (AD 717–720), advertises humiliating and debilitating conditions on the non-Muslims: they were excluded from public office, their dress was prescribed and could not equal that of a Muslim, they could ride asses or mules but not horses, their houses had to be humbler than Muslim ones, and they could repair their places of worship only with permission but could not build new ones. They were not allowed to display visible signs of their faith (such as crosses), nor were they permitted to use bells which could be heard outside. A Christian's testimony against a Muslim was unacceptable in the courts and if a Muslim killed a non-Muslim, the penalty was a fine. They must pay the *jizya* in person and in a way which revealed their subject status. They should always give way to a Muslim in the street and not sell anything forbidden to Muslims in places where a Muslim might see them, and so on.[86]

For the early Arab Muslims some arrangement such as the *dhimma* was essential. A relatively small number of them had very quickly gained vast territories with large non-Muslim populations. It was in their interest to ensure that such populations remained both subject and productive. The *dhimma* was a means of bringing this about. The dilemma for the modern student is that the *dhimma*

---

86   Hitti, *History of the Arabs*, p. 234; Nazir-Ali, *Islam*, p. 38; and Ye'or, *The Dhimmi*, p. 169. Ye'or shows how at least some of these provisions came to characterize the *dhimma* down the years.

represents both an advance and a problem. It is an advance in that it regulated the treatment of people whose beliefs differed from those of the rulers. At a time when even such limited tolerance was rare, it allowed at least some of these communities to survive and even to prosper. It is a problem because from time to time the full rigour of its provisions was invoked, though there were other periods of history when it was not. It is also a problem because there are significant groups in the Muslim world who, in their desire to enforce what they see as the Sharī'a, or Islamic Law, want to treat non-Muslims as *dhimmīs* rather than as equal citizens. In some countries, there are laws already giving effect to such desires.

Certainly, the *dhimma* should be studied for the lessons which can be learnt from its history. As we shall see, these can be both positive and negative. It should not, however, be taken in isolation as the only historical model available for the regulation of relationships between Muslims and non-Muslims. Other models, such as the Constitution of Medīna, mentioned already, and at least some understandings of the *Dār ul-Sulh*, where Muslims and non-Muslims live peaceably together by agreement, need also to be further studied.[87] It should also be noted that in most contemporary polities, non-Muslims and Muslims are both citizens with equal responsibilities, freedoms and opportunities.

---

87 See further the article on 'Dār Al-Sulh' in *Encyclopaedia of Islam*, Brill, Leiden, 1953.

THE DEVELOPMENT OF
ISLAMIC CIVILIZATION

In spite of the *dhimma* and the restrictions which were
imposed by it, Jews, Christians, Zoroastians and others col-
laborated with Muslims in a whole range of intellectual,
cultural and scientific activities which led to the development of what is known as classical Islamic civilization. At
first, the new empire was dependent on using the languages
of the previous empires, Roman or Persian, for its official
transactions. It was not until the reign of the Umayyad
Caliph 'Abd Al-Malik (AD 685–705) that Greek and
Persian ceased being official languages and were replaced by
Arabic. Even in the development of *fiqh*, as represented in
the emergence of the different *madhāhib* or schools of law,
scholars have seen the influence, variously, of Roman and
Persian law. Even many of the most notable Muslims of the
early period were not of Arab origin at all: Nizām al-Mulk
was the great Turkish vizier of the Abbaside period; Al-
Ghazzālī, the greatest theologian Islām has ever known, was
of Persian origin, as was the scientist and philosopher Ibn
Sīnā or Avicenna; whereas the political theorist, Al-Farābī
was of Turkish stock. In different ways, then, the various
civilizations which had been brought within the domains of
Islām made their distinctive contributions. As Hitti remarks
this was another instance of the victors made 'captive by
the vanquished'.[88]

The Christians within the Empire made perhaps their
most memorable contribution in the acquisition, study and
translation of Greek philosophical, medical and scientific
work into Arabic, usually through Syriac. Much of this

---

88   Hitti, *History of the Arabs*, p. 174.

work took place under the patronage of the Abbaside Caliphs, some of whom at least had an interest in the reconciliation between revelation and reason. The Christians themselves came from different traditions: there were Jacobites, Melkites, Nestorians and Maronites among them. An outstanding example, in this connection, is the father and son team of the Nestorians Hunayn Ibn Isḥāq and Isḥāq Ibn Hunayn. Between them they are said to have translated the whole of the curriculum of the medical school at Alexandria, besides translations of Plato and Aristotle and much else. Their *modus operandi* seems to have been that the father would translate from Greek into Syriac and then the son, who was the better Arabist, would translate into Arabic. Because of them, much Greek medical knowledge, which would otherwise have been lost, has been preserved in Arabic. Muslim philosophers and physicians, jurists and theologians studied, commented upon and improved on this vast heritage. Gradually, this learning seeped into Western Europe, mainly through the efforts of Jewish traders who also sometimes were the translators into Latin.[89] Its influence on the recovery of learning, and the eventual Renaissance, is difficult to over-estimate.

There was, of course, vigorous interaction in the worlds of art and architecture, of maritime enterprise and of strategic technology, but perhaps the most fascinating is the constant interaction in theology. We have seen already how, from the earliest period, Christians and Muslims were in contact with one another and how there was a vigorous discussion of religious ideas and doctrines. Such has remained the case throughout history, but it may be that the

---

89 Nazir-Ali, *Islam*, pp. 70f; Hitti, *History of the Arabs*, pp. 309f; Walzer, *Greek into Arabic* (as note 68); and O'Leary, *Greek Science* (as note 68).

impulse for the development of formal theology in Islām specifically came from the Christian sources which were also involved in mediating Greek philosophical ideas. Theology in Islām came to be called *Kalām*, and this is not without significance, for the relation of God to his speech became one of the central concerns of theology in Islām. For the orthodox party, as represented by Al-Ash'arī, the speech of God is eternal, whereas for the Mu'tazila or the Rationalist such a belief would compromise the unity of God. Behind the discussion we can discern not only the ways in which the Muslim scriptures describe the qualities of God, but also Greek philosophical ideas and, above all, Christian notions of the relations between the Persons of the Trinity.[90] Among the Shī'a, there are parallels with Christian concerns in matters of divine mediation through human agency, and also most importantly in a positive evaluation of suffering.

EARLY EXAMPLES OF DIALOGUE

There seems to have been a real difference of approach between Christians who lived within the Islamic world and those who did not. The polemical dominates for a considerable period in northern Europe and even in Byzantium. Attempts are made to show the new faith in the worst possible light. This is quite different from the position adopted, for instance, by St John of Damascus who had been a close friend of the Umayyad Caliphs and had,

---

90   Nazir-Ali, *Islam*, pp. 66ff; Hitti, *History of the Arabs*, pp. 245f. Also J. W. Sweetman's masterly *Islam and Christian Theology*, Vols 1–4, Lutterworth, London, 1945–67.

indeed, held the highest office, that of financial adminis-
trator, in the Caliphate. He gave it all up to enter the
monastery of St Sāba near Jerusalem. John, famously,
regarded Islām as a kind of Judaeo–Christian heresy but was
also concerned to be fair, for example, in how he understood the Qur'ān. In his surviving dialogue with a Muslim,
there is a discussion about the divinity of Christ. The
argument proceeds on the basis that each side knows the
Scripture of the other. The Qur'ān, according to John,
refers to Jesus as word and spirit of God. These must be
eternal, as we cannot imagine God to be without speech
and spirit. If they are eternal, they must be God, or we have
acknowledged three separate 'eternals' and this is really the
sin of *shirk* or of associating partners with God (for Muslims,
this is the worst sin imaginable). There is, first of all, an
awareness throughout this argument of the Muslim discussion about exactly how the attributes of God related to the
divine essence. There is then an acknowledgement of some
commonality of belief, for instance, belief in God's unity,
from which the dialogue can proceed.

Similarly, Theodore Abū Qurrāh (d. AD 820), the Bishop
of Harrān, attempts to explain the doctrine of the Trinity by
appealing to the Muslim view that the various scriptures
revealed to the Prophets and Apostles all come from the
same *Lawh Al-Mahfūz* (Preserved Tablet) or *Umm Al-Kitāb*
(Mother of the Book). They are, therefore, one and yet
demonstrably distinct. Abū Qurrāh also attempts to meet
Muslim claims that Islām has superseded Judaism and Christianity by saying that such supersession would have been
attended by irresistible signs and wonders (we know that
this was a common Jewish objection in the time of the
Prophet himself). The definitive Muslim response then was
to point to the miracle, *i'jāz* of the Qur'ān itself (2:23,

10:38, etc.). There was also important contact regarding the freedom of the will and the relationship of reason to revelation, which affected future attitudes among Muslims, for example, to philosophy.[91]

John and Theodore were both Melkites, that is, from the Chalcedonian Orthodox Churches. By contrast, Timothy, Patriarch of Baghdad at the time of the Abbaside Al-Mahdī, the father of the famous Hārūn Ar-Rashīd, was the head of the Assyrian Church of the East or the 'Nestorians' as they are commonly known but do not much like. The Nestorians were sometimes well liked by Muslims because they did not have images in their churches, used plain crosses instead of crucifixes, and whilst believing that Christ was divine, they distinguished between his divine and human nature. Also, they did not refer to the Blessed Virgin as Theotokos or God-bearer, strictly speaking, but quite often simply translated 'Mother of God'. This could come out in Arabic as *Umm Allah* or, as in the Coptic liturgy, at least, as *Wālidat Al-ilah* (either Mother of Allah or Mother of the God).

Timothy's dialogues with the Caliph have survived and have been published. They are a model of the courtesy and good relations which seem to have existed between the two men. Timothy prays publicly for the Caliph and asks God's blessing on him, but there is no hint of a compromise where matters of belief are concerned. The dialogues are full, frank and fair. They cover a wide range of topics, including the Incarnation. Timothy shows that he is aware of the Christology of the Qur'ān and, indeed, appeals to it for support!

---

91   Richard Bell, *The Origin of Islam in its Christian Environment*, Frank Cass, London, 1968, pp. 207ff; Nazir-Ali, *Frontiers* (as note 68), pp. 17ff; Hitti, *History of the Arabs*, p. 245; John V. Tolan (ed.), *Medieval Christian Perceptions of Islam*, Routledge, New York, 2000.

The death of Christ by crucifixion and its necessarily public nature is also discussed (Timothy reveals here how the Nestorians continued the Antiochene tradition, and especially that of Theodore of Mopsuestia). The Trinity is explained, with Timothy's famous allegory of the sun with its light and heat; the heat and light are one with the sun but also have their own distinctive modes of being, and not only of manifestation. So also the Son and the Spirit are one with the Father but also distinctive in their being and doing. The integrity of the Bible is demonstrated by the mutual hostility of the Jews and the Christians: if either changed the older Testament in the slightest, the other would point it out. As far as the New is concerned, all the churches, in spite of their differences, agree on it and no one has attempted to smooth out the difficulties and apparent contradictions. He also challenges the Muslims to produce an 'uncorrupted' Gospel, if they believed the New Testament to be corrupt (which seems to be indirect evidence that Muslim versions of the Gospel such as that of 'Barnabas' did not exist at the time).[92]

MONKS AND MYSTICS

One area of interaction which we cannot ignore is the emergence of mysticism, *Tasawwuf* or Sūfism, in Islām. There is more and more of a consensus among scholars that the roots of this are to be found in the experience of the Prophet himself and in the Qur'ān. The beautiful 'throne verse' of the Qur'ān, which speaks of God's *kursī* or throne

---

92   See further William Young, *Patriarch, Shah and Caliph*, Christian Study Centre, Rawalpindi, 1974, pp. 133f. and 198ff.

extending throughout the heavens and the earth (2:255), or the famous 'light-verse', which is about God being the light of the heavens and the earth (24:35), are quite often taken to be examples of a mystical sense in the Qur'ān. They were particular favourites of the Sūfīs, who loved finding 'mystic' or inner meaning in them. The best known example of this must be Al-Ghazzālī's *Mishkāt-ul-Anwār*, or the Niche of Lights. Here a distinction is made between the physical world where we see by the light of the sun, and the spiritual where we see by revelation. The Prophets are the lamps which are lit by the pure light of God, who is self-existent light, and not kindled by another light. These lamps then diffuse the divine light in the world around them.[93] As we have seen in Chapter 1, the verse itself suggests something like a Christian sanctuary-lamp being used as imagery. From his sojourns in Syria and elsewhere, the Prophet of Islām may well have been familiar with such lamps.

Another passage in the Qur'ān which suggests a mystic consciousness is that of the night-journey to the 'Farthest Mosque' when the Prophet is said to have travelled through the heavens (17:1). There is already an account in the earliest *Sīrah* but the passage, understandably, has attracted much comment and development down the years. Similarly, the Sūra in the Qur'ān which tells of the one who taught Muhammad coming 'two bow-lengths or nearer' is regarded, particularly by the Sūfīs, as referring to union with the Divine Beloved (53:9).

The great Sūfī teacher and expositor, and founder of the Whirling Dervishes, Maulānā Jalāluddīn Rūmī, tells us in his preface to the second book of the Mathnawī (sometimes known as the Bible in Persian) that God's love is primary,

---

93 Trans. W. H. T. Gairdner, Royal Asiatic Society, London, 1924.

whereas our love is derivative. It is only God's grace which makes it possible for us to love God and our fellow human beings. He refers to 5:57, where it is said that God loves the believers, *yuhibbuhum* and they, in turn, love him *yuhibbunahu*. *Mahabba*, in fact, continued to be the ordinary Sūfī word for love of God until it was replaced by the more passionate *'ishq*.

There seem to have been ascetical tendencies among the close companions of the Prophet (the *Sahāba*), and teachers of mysticism had emerged in both Shī'a and Sunnī Islām within the first two centuries.[94] There is also general agreement, however, that, whatever the original impulses, Sūfism also developed in interaction with Christianity. Both Muhammad Iqbāl and Margaret Smith have drawn our attention to the contact, influence and dialogue between the early Sūfīs and the Christian monks of the deserts of Syria and Egypt. As we have noted in discussing the rise of Sūfism, Iqbāl identifies a number of factors. To remind you, these are, *inter alia*, the political unrest which became characteristic of the late Umayyad and early Abbaside period; the scepticism of rationalism which led to the search for a super-intellectual source of knowledge; the legalism encouraged by the law-schools; encounter with people of different faiths; moral laxity brought about by increasing prosperity; and, finally, 'the presence of Christianity as a working ideal of life'. Again, for Iqbāl it was the actual life of the monks which influenced the Sūfīs, rather than their theological beliefs. In this connection, it may be worth mentioning that Metropolitan Anthony of Sourozh

94 See further Nazir-Ali, 'Love and Law' (as note 14), pp. 321ff; J. Spencer Trimingham, *The Sufi Orders in Islam*, OUP, Oxford, 1971, p. 2; and the article on 'Tasawwuf' in *Encyclopaedia of Islam*. See also Anne-Marie Schimmel's magisterial *Mystical Dimensions of Islam* (as note 16).

tells us that God's condescending love and the response which this elicits in the believer was a leading concern of the desert fathers.[95] We know that this was also the case with leading Sūfīs.

The Sūfīs are known to have regarded Jesus as the pattern of ascetical and mystical life. They emphasized his poverty in total dedication to God, and also his purity. His powers of healing, even raising the dead, are often mentioned. It is no wonder that contemporary Christians have found at least some kinds of Sūfism congenial. The great evangelical Anglican layman, Sir Norman Anderson, who was also a leading Islamic scholar, regarded Rābi'a Al-Addawiyya, one of the first Sūfī 'saints' and a woman, as well as Ibrāhīm ibn Adham, an early Sūfī from Balkh in Afghanistan, as examples of those in whom the Holy Spirit was working. He felt that such people would either be vouchsafed the message of forgiveness and peace in this life, like Cornelius in the early Church, or they would realize who it was that had saved them on the other side of the grave.[96] It is interesting that these are the reflections, not of a pluralist, but of one who firmly believed in the uniqueness of Christ and the value of his atoning death. He believed that those who responded to the promptings of the Holy Spirit by seeking and knocking on the door would have the door opened to them and they would find the desire of their heart.[97]

---

95   Iqbāl, *The Development of Metaphysics in Persia* (as note 15), pp. 76ff; Margaret Smith, *Studies in Early Mysticism in the Near and Middle-East*, London, 1931; and Benedicta Ward (ed.), *The Sayings of the Desert Fathers*, Mowbray, Oxford, 1981, pp. viif.
96   J. N. D. Anderson, *God's Law and God's Love: An Essay in Comparative Religion*, Collins, London, p. 128.
97   J. N. D. Anderson, *Christianity and Comparative Religion*, Tyndale, London, 1970, pp. 100ff.

It is true, of course, that both Sūfism and Christian mysticism have been prone to similar errors and to the dangers stemming from them, whether in an excess of asceticism, separation from the community or spiritual pride. Both have been exposed to the temptations of monism and of pantheism, and yet both at their best can be fully holistic, even if sometimes in a panentheistic form. An example of this is 'Allāma Iqbāl, the poet-philosopher of Pakistan, who, in his lectures on the reconstruction of Islamic thought, took a pampsychist and panentheistic position: he held that God was the Ultimate Ego from whom only egos proceeded. Every atom of divine energy, however low in the scale of being, was an ego of sorts. Throughout the entire gamut of being runs the gradually rising note of ego-hood, until it reaches its perfection in the human. Conflating Paul's speech at Athens with Rūmī at this point, his understanding of the universe is that 'like pearls do we live and move and have our being in the perpetual flow of Divine Life'.[98]

TURKS, MONGOLS AND INFIDELS

There were, of course, local rebellions, treachery and civil wars to disturb this feast of reason and flow of soul, but the Abbaside paradise was brought to an end by huge movements of people which were difficult even to comprehend, let alone to match. At first these were the Turkic

---

98 M. Iqbāl, *The Reconstruction of Religious Thought in Islam*, Ashraf, Lahore, 1971, pp. 71ff; (cf Acts 17:28); Maulānā Jalāluddīn Rūmī, *Kulliyāt-i-Shams-i-Tabrīzī*, M. Dervish (ed.), Tehran 1341 H.S., Vol. 3, p. 76; and M. Iqbāl's own *Rumūz-i-Bēkhūdī*, Lahore, 1918.

peoples, recently Islamicized through Iran, who poured into the Anatolian region of the Eastern Empire and began to threaten both Byzantium and Baghdad. They overran Syria and Palestine. In due course, even the Caliph became a figurehead while the Turks ruled much of the Islamic Empire. In fact, the Abbasides never regained their position until the Ottomans assumed the trappings and title of Caliph sometime in the sixteenth century.[99]

The Turkish invasions were also one of the presenting reasons for the Crusades. It had become highly unsafe for pilgrims to travel through Asia Minor to the Holy Land, and something had to be done for their security. The anger of all Christians, Eastern and Western, had been kindled by the wanton destruction of the Holy Sepulchre by the mad Fātimid Al-Hākim (who later turned on the Muslims). Most importantly, the Eastern Emperor, Alexius Comnenus, had appealed directly to Pope Urban II for help as the Asian part of his Empire was being overrun by the Seljūks. All of this was in Urban's mind as he preached the call to what became the first Crusade.[100] The history of the Crusades is too well known to need repetition here, save to say that there were many ebbs and flows in the fortunes of the different sides. There were periods of truce and even of cordiality. There was much bravery and chivalry on all sides. Some of the Crusaders behaved like marauding barbarians and their behaviour, for instance, in the taking of Jerusalem, is reprehensible and inexcusable. These were, however, violent times, and outrages cannot be placed only at the doors of the Crusaders. In different ways and at

---

99   Hitti, *History of the Arabs*, pp. 633ff.
100   For an account of the Crusades see Runciman's comprehensive *History of the Crusades* (as note 38).

different times there were massacres, enslavement and treachery perpetrated on all sides. It is certainly wrong to compare the worst of Islām with the best of Christianity; but it is equally mistaken to compare the worst of Christianity with the best of Islām. This is done sometimes when the story of the Crusades is told.

From the Muslim point of view, the Crusades are certainly viewed with much bitterness, but it appears that contemporary Muslim chronicles did not refer to them as religious wars, but as wars waged by the Franks, much as they might have discussed wars waged by the Turks or Mongols. There are stories in the Muslim accounts as well of friendships, tolerance, justice and a desire for peace on both sides.[101] It may be worth pointing out again that the Crusades were not waged merely against the Muslims. Eastern Christians and Jews suffered perhaps the most at the hands of both the Crusaders and Muslim rulers or populations.[102] There was even a Crusade directed specifically at Constantinople,[103] and a particularly nasty one that targeted the Jews of Central Europe.[104] There were Crusades against the Albigensian heretics, and even against enemies of the Pope.[105] There were demands that the wars against Protestants should be declared Crusades, even though they never quite achieved that status.[106]

Because of its use in the Islamic world to denote

---

101   For such a view of the Crusades see Maalouf, *The Crusades Through Arab Eyes* (as note 39).
102   Runciman, *History of the Crusades*, Vol. I, p. 294, Vol. III, p. 446.
103   *Ibid.*, Vol. III, pp. 107ff.
104   *Ibid.*, Vol. I, pp. 134ff.
105   *Ibid.*, Vol. III, p. 339.
106   See further Chadwick, *The Reformation* (as note 37), pp. 365ff.

barbarism, aggression and Islamophobia, and in the West to mean charitable or evangelistic movements, the word 'crusade' has acquired highly ambivalent and dangerous sets of meanings. It is desirable, therefore, to demythologize the term and the events to which it refers. It is important to place them within a historical frame of reference and to understand the political and socio-economic, as well as religious, forces which led to them. Western Christians should certainly be prepared to repudiate the excesses committed by the Crusaders; but all of us, as partners in dialogue, should be prepared to repent of the wrongs we have done one another, often in the name of religion. At the same time, we should ensure that history will not determine our relations today.

For more than two hundred years, the Turks and the Mongols continued to ravage the ancient civilizations of the East and to threaten Europe. At the same time, leadership in the Islamic world had passed to non-Arabs, be they Kurds, Turkomans or Mamelukes. It is in this context that the periodic attacks by the Mongols are to be seen. When they pillaged and destroyed Baghdad in 1258, it was only the most horrific example of their destruction of a number of cities in the Muslim world. The Muslim historians describe the capture of the city in apocalyptic terms, as do the poets. This is how the twelfth-century Arab historian Ibn Al-Athīr saw it: 'The events I am about to describe are so horrible that for years I avoided all mention of them. It is not easy to announce that death has fallen upon Islām and the Muslims. Alas! I would have preferred my mother never to have given birth to me, or to have died without witnessing all these evils. If one day you are told that the earth has never known such calamity since God created Adam, do not hesitate to believe it, for such is the strict truth.'[107] In strikingly similar language, the Persian poet Sa'adī refers to the fall of Baghdad as the Day of Judgement:

'O Muhammad! If you are to raise your head from the dust on Judgement Day; Raise your head now and see judgement in the midst of creation!' (My translation). There seems to be evidence that the Mongols were most severe on Sunnī Muslims and least on the Shi'a and Nestorian Christians. This was because they had extensive Shi'a and Nestorian contacts; indeed, there were Nestorians among them.[108]

The Crusades and petty in-fighting among the different Muslim rulers had left the Islamic world without a focus of unity. The Caliph was but a puppet of the Mameluke Sultans in Egypt. Eastern Christianity, and particularly Byzantium, was also weakened by the Crusades and by the plotting of the European city-states in particular. It seemed that the time was right for a new power to arise. The Mongols could only consolidate themselves in India, where the Mughal Empire flourished for centuries. In the Middle and Near East, however, an obscure Turkish tribe called 'Uthmān or Osmān began to establish itself on both sides of the Sea of Marmara. In spite of setbacks, it was destined to replace not only whatever was left of an Arab Caliphate, but also to conquer Constantinople and to replace the Eastern Roman Empire. It was to expand into the Balkans and was only to be checked at the very gates of Vienna. The

---

107 *Al-Kāmil fi'l-Tārīkh*, quoted in Maalouf, *The Crusades Through Arab Eyes*, p. 235.

108 Hitti, *History of the Arabs*, pp. 485 and 701ff; Maalouf, *The Crusades Through Arab Eyes*, pp. 235ff; on Mongol contacts with the Nestorians see E. A. Wallis Budge, *The Monks of Kublai Khan*, Religious Tract Society, 1928.

Turk now replaced the Arab as the enemy most feared by Europe. From the fifteenth to the nineteenth century, the Ottomans ruled not only most of the Arab world but also significant areas of Europe. Within their territories were large numbers of Jews and Christians and they had to devise systems to cope with the sheer heterogeneity of their Empire.[109]

One point, made by Philip Hitti, which is perhaps worth noting, is that the numerous Central Asian peoples who poured into the Middle and Near East, whether Turk or Mongol, Seljūk or Ottoman, submitted eventually to Islām; a culture, polity and religion they had come to destroy. This reveals the ability of Islām not only to assimilate subjugated peoples over a period of time, but even those who come as conquerors. This is a factor which must be taken into account in any assessment of contemporary Islām.[110]

---

109   Runciman, *History of the Crusades*, Vol. III, pp. 452ff; Hitti, *History of the Arabs*, pp. 701ff.
110   See further Hitti, *History of the Arabs*, p. 475.

4

Liberation, Nationalism and Islamism

Whenever I visit the country of Turkey, I feel that I am confronted by a paradox: on the one hand, I find a modern, monoglot and largely monocultural nation and, on the other, there are remains, whether Hellenistic, Roman, Byzantine or even Ottoman, of great plural civilizations.

We have seen how the emergent Ottomans came to preside over a great diversity of people belonging to a whole range of ethnic and religious groups. Eventually the empire was to contain not only Arabs and Arabized populations of the Fertile Crescent, but Persians, Greeks, Slavs, Armenians and others. Every kind of Christianity was included: Syrian, Assyrian, Greek, Armenian, Monophysite, Nestorian, Uniate and even Latin. How was such a vast multitude to be governed?

There were, of course, centralizing, despotic and tyrannical episodes in the four hundred years of Ottoman ascendancy; but there were also, perhaps more characteristically, periods where a high degree of autonomy of the subject peoples was recognized, or at least tolerated. This was true, at various times, in the Balkans, in Egypt, in Syria and in the Lebanon.[111] It was, however, in the Ottoman use

---

111   *The Cambridge History of Islam* (as note 83), Vol. 1A, pp. 354ff.

and development of the so-called *millet* system that their inventiveness is most clearly shown.

Bishop William Young has shown, in his ground-breaking work *Patriarch, Shah and Caliph*, how the *millet* system was first developed by the Persian Sassanians in regulating the place of the Church of the East (later to be known as the Assyrian or Nestorian Church) within the Persian Empire. When the Muslims conquered Persia, this idea was assimilated to the *dhimma*, but it was the Ottomans who refined it and used it most extensively.[112] While the *dhimma* was supposed to be applied uniformly for all *dhimmī* communities whether they be Zoroastrians, Christians of different kinds, or Jews; in fact demographic, geographical, economic and political factors had to be taken into account in each case. Each *millet* was required to be strongly cohesive and to meet its economic and fiscal needs while also contributing to the empire as a whole. Individuals and families, clans and villages were protected by belonging to a *millet* recognized by the Muslim authorities. They had their own ecclesiastical heads who also functioned as liaison with the Ottomans. Their courts had jurisdiction in the areas of trade as well as personal and family law, and their notables had enormous power both within their communities and, sometimes, more widely than that. Such an arrangement created, in due course, a mentality which could be both inward-looking *and* servile towards the rulers.[113]

The high profile autonomy of the *millets*, the claims of regional rulers and the tendency, therefore, to fragment remain features of those parts of the world which were

---

112　Young, *Patriarch, Shah and Caliph* (as note 92), pp. 27ff.
113　See further Cragg, *The Arab Christian* (as note 60), pp. 114ff; Ye'or, *The Decline of Eastern Christianity* (as note 60), pp. 224ff.

under Ottoman domination. In the present international situation, whether in the Balkans or in the Middle East, it is important to recognize this historical factor and to work with the grain in this respect rather than against it. This may argue for the evolution of dispensations which are 'federal' or even 'con-federal' rather than unitary, and in which ethnic, linguistic and religious identities are recognized and affirmed rather than neglected or denied. While geography is important, any federal approach worth its name must take these factors into account.

FROM *DHIMMI* TO CITIZEN

Because of increasing military and commercial contact between the Ottomans and Western (as well as Russian) interests, pressure grew for improvement in the status of the large Christian, Jewish and other minorities within the Ottoman world. Many of the Christian-majority regions had already acquired a degree of self-government, but this was not seen as enough. In a series of edicts, beginning with Sultan 'Abdul-Majid's Khatt-i-Sherīf of Gulhane (1839) and culminating in the *firmān* known as the *Khatt-i-Humāyūn* (1856), the *dhimmī* condition was first modified and ameliorated and then abolished altogether. Non-Muslims were now assured religious liberty and equality in the areas of justice, taxation, employment and access to civil and military service. It is important to note that these changes were made by progressive sultans and a small vanguard of their supporters, even though the tide of Muslim opinion was against them and the 'Ulemā were hostile.

Paradoxically, even the non-Muslim communities were

not wholly enthusiastic about their newly acquired status. There was a threat to their cohesiveness in the freshly promulgated arrangements, and their notables, both clerical and lay, feared the loss of privilege. Many of the Christians were not keen to be recruited into the armed forces as they would have had to fight other Christians, perhaps struggling for their independence. Western powers (and Russia) were also unwilling to forgo privileges they enjoyed, for example, through the system of capitulations which gave them trading concessions as well as the right to employ local Christians as their agents. Gradually, many non-Muslim communities had become clients of Western powers and expected protection in return. They were unwilling to lose such protection for an unknown future.[114] As Bat Ye'or has repeatedly observed, there is such a thing as a *dhimmī* mentality which hardly recognizes its tattered and captive state and is grateful for small mercies.

THE RISE OF NATIONALISM

The reforms of the *Tanzīmāt* (as they were collectively known) were very far-reaching. They extended to commercial and penal law and even sought to restrict the application of the Sharī'a to personal and family matters. One of their consequences was to give rise to democratic aspirations and, when these were suppressed, to those of separation, especially among the Arab subjects of the empire. The tale of their alienation from the Ottomans is only too well known and it is true that the Great Powers of

---

114 See Cragg, *The Arab Christian*, pp. 122ff, 145ff; Ye'or, *The Decline of Eastern Christianity*, p. 226; and *The Cambridge History of Islam*, p. 366.

the day saw in this an opportunity to further their own interests in the region. It is ironic that these reforms signalled the beginning of the end of the Ottomans. Christian-inspired nationalisms were already in the air in the Balkans. There was, however, now the emergence of a sense of Arab identity and pride which was to be reckoned with. The so-called *Nahda*, or Renaissance, certainly had political implications which were gradually worked out in terms of independence; but there were important cultural and spiritual aspects to it as well.

One of the remarkable features of the *Nahda* is the contribution made to its articulation, development and propagation by Christian Arabs (on the whole, the large Jewish communities of the Arab world did not participate in it). The Ottoman reforms had given the Christians a new *locus standi* whereby they were no longer *dhimmī* but co-citizens with the Muslims. In fact, Christians were freer than Muslims (who were still bound by religious ties to the Ottoman Caliph) to articulate this new sense of Arab-ness. Writers like Constantine Zurayq and George Antonius initiated vigorous debates on the nature of Arab-ness, in relation to Islām and its literary and cultural heritage.[115] One area of discussion for both Christians and Muslims was the role of religion in the political sphere. Some wanted to restrict it to the personal sphere, but others were aware of its history and were prepared to concede some role for Islām, in particular in the affairs of state. Earlier thinking about Arab-ness in its cultural, spiritual and political manifestations was, however, to give way to the development of largely secular nationalist ideologies. The emergence of the Ba'ath Party in Syria and Iraq is an example of this

---

115   Cragg, *The Arab Christian*, pp. 153ff.

tendency. It is interesting, in this connection, to note that its inspiration and leadership came from people like Michel 'Aflaq, who was from a Syrian Christian background and who, in exile in Iraq, was accorded precedence even over Saddam Hussein!

Egypt also provides an example of nationalism during this period, but here there is much greater consciousness of Egypt's own past; its Pharaonic and Coptic history. As far as this has been the case, the Copts have been able to contribute especially to nationalist movements which have had a strong 'Egyptian' rather than merely 'Arab' flavour. As early as the beginning of the twentieth century, it was possible for Egypt to have a Christian Prime Minister, Butrus Ghālī, even if he was assassinated by extremists. We have seen already how the secular nationalism of the PLO looked to a unitary state in which Muslims, Christians and Jews could live together. Once again, many of the ideologues of Palestinian nationalism have been Christian. For some certainly, the Arabicization of Christians whether in culture, language or political aspiration, is yet another sign of the servility induced by their prolonged status as *dhimmī* and only serves the cause of continued Muslim hegemony. For others, though, it heralds a new status as citizens, even if not always equal, with the possibility of genuinely contributing to nation-building.

Arab nationalism was not, of course, the only nationalism to emerge during this period. The contraction of the Ottoman empire into a largely Asian and Turk dominated territory was accompanied by a form of Turkish nationalism which looked for solidarity not towards its former domains in East or West, but to the people of Turkic origin in Central Asia. Its chief ideologue was Ziyā Gökalp (1875–1924). Ziyā also recognized Islām as a feature of

Turkish heritage but sought to combine it with folk-memory and far-reaching westernization. In this context, instead of non-Muslims contributing to nationalism, they were, rather, restricted by it. Their growing discontent resulted in persecution, deportation and massacres. It is this which gives modern Turkey its monolithic character.

In India, Muslims began to sense, more and more, that their identity and distinctiveness would be inevitably compromised in an undivided and independent India where the Hindus would be a dominant and unchecked majority. Repeated refusals by the Indian National Congress to consider Muslim concerns in an adequate way led to demands for more and more autonomy and, ultimately, for complete independence. 'Allāma Iqbāl, the philosopher-poet and chief ideologue for a separate Muslim state in the sub-continent, was consistent in his demand for full autonomy, and eventually brought Muhammad Ali Jinnah, or the Quāid-i-A'zam (the Great Leader) as he is known today, the founder of Pakistan, around to his point of view. Deteriorating relations between the communities, as well as bad feeling among their leaders, also contributed to the division. It is the case, however, that the situation was very finely balanced until the last minute and could possibly have been retrieved.[116] Mr George Felix, a Pakistani Christian, has shown how the Christian political leadership, especially of the Punjab, supported the Muslim League in its final demand for partition. Indeed, it can be said that Pakistan became a viable entity as a result of the Christian

---

116 See further Akbar Ahmed, *Jinnah, Pakistan and Islamic Identity,* Routledge, London, 1947, pp. 61ff; Sheila McDonough, *The Flame of Sinai: Hope and Vision in Iqbal,* Iqbāl Academy, Lahore, 2002, pp. 99ff; *The Cambridge History of Islam,* Vol. 2A, pp. 107ff.

vote. The thinking of the Christian leaders seems to have been based on the view that one oppressed minority should support another, and that Christians could expect a better deal from the Muslims than from the Hindus and Sikhs. In the early years of Independence this perception seemed vindicated, but George Felix's book is really about how nationalist aspiration and fair treatment of minorities was sacrificed to an emerging theocratic ideology which had been very far from the minds of the founders of Pakistan.[117] In fact, many of those who had espoused the theocracy had also been opposed to the creation of Pakistan, on the grounds that the movement was led by secularized Muslims who did not intend to establish a truly Islamic state and that partition would divide the Muslim presence in the sub-continent.

HOW ISLAMISM HAS REPLACED NATIONALISM

The retreat of nationalist ideology in the face of a rapidly advancing 'Islamist' ideology in Pakistan is only an example of a much wider phenomenon in the Islamic world. The secularizing politics of Nasserism, Ba'athism and the left-leaning nationalisms of Algeria and the PLO were rejected in favour of a radical and comprehensive Islām. It is true that the new economic power of some of the Gulf States encouraged the emergence of radically conservative forms of Islām, and that the Islamic revolution in Iran gave Islamic activists hope that their aims were achievable. This

---

117 George Felix, *Quaid-E-Azam's Vision: Christians in Pakistan*, Agape, Salford, 2001, pp. 18ff.

is, however, only part of the story, as the roots of these movements are, on the one hand, very deep and, on the other, represent significant demographic shifts in today's world.

There is a tendency in most religious thought to appeal to the past. Such a tendency is also quite pronounced in Islām, and is characteristic of both 'progressive' and 'conservative' thinking. Ebrahim Moosa, the South African Muslim leader, claims that this is because Muslim legal and ethical thought proceeds on an analogical basis (that of *qiyās*) and attempts to map the present and future in terms of the past. What is proposed for the present or the future can only be legitimized if a precedent, however remote, can be found. This makes it susceptible to utopias, real or imagined, from the past, rather than the development of dynamic principles which work in the present.[118] Whatever the truth of this observation, we certainly find in many Sunnī Islamist movements a line running from Ibn Hanbal through Ibn Taimiyya to 'Abdul Wahhāb. The first is one of the four, and the most conservative, eponymous founders of the Sunnī law schools or *madhāhib*. His school relies almost entirely on the sayings and practice of the Prophet, rather than on the development of legal processes in the light of actual circumstances.[119] Where Ibn Taimiyya is concerned, Fazlur Rahman's judgement is that his aim was to rediscover and reconstitute the early normative community of Islām. He railed against 'accretions' in Muslim society which he blamed on the influence of Christian communities in

---

118   In Fazlur Rahmān's *Revival and Reform in Islam* (E. Moosa, ed.), Oxford, Oneworld, 2000, pp. 204ff.
119   See further the assessment in Wael B. Hallaq's *Authority, Continuity and Change in Islamic Law*, CUP, Cambridge, 2001, pp. 39f.

Muslim lands: it was his work which inspired the icono-clasm of the Wahhābīs in their destruction of shrines, both Shīʿa and Sūfī, and their attempt to establish a theocratic state in the Arabian Peninsula.[120] Later militants, however, were to label even the official Wahhābists of Saʿūdī Arabia as compromised, and they sought to practice a *Salafī* form of faith which took the sacred text in its most literal sense. They were hostile to any innovation and wished for a return to a primitive and pure form of Islām.[121]

While it is important to consider the theological and his-torical roots of Islamism, it is also necessary to take account of the socio-economic contexts. Here we find a situation where a population explosion in many Muslim countries had created a large, young and male section of the community which was relatively well educated, or at least literate, but was also frustrated. Many of these young people had only a tenuous grip on Islamic tradition as a whole. The preponderance of technical, scientific and medical qualifi-cations among their leadership has often been noticed. These factors left them open to determined and well-financed indoctrination whether from a *Salafī* or Shīʿa point of view.[122]

---

120   Rahmān, *Revival and Reform*, pp. 132ff; Malise Ruthven, *A Fury for God: the Islamic Attack on America*, Granta, London, 2002, pp. 135ff.
121   Gilles Kepel, *Jihād: The Trail of Political Islam*, I B Tauris, London, 2003, pp. 219ff.
122   Kepel, *Jihād*, pp. 65ff; Ruthven, *A Fury for God*, pp. 113ff.

THE REJECTION OF COLONIALISM AND NEO-COLONIALISM

Somewhat paradoxically, their very lack of grounding in a well-rounded tradition was a factor in their adoption of the highly selective reading of Islām promoted by the activists. The rise of Islamism has to be evaluated in the light of other factors as well. One of the most important, undoubtedly, is the experience of imperialism, whether western or Ottoman. Towards the end of the nineteenth century, both were displaying secularizing agendas and both had sympathizers, but also opponents, in the Muslim world. The famous debate between Sir Syed Ahmad Khan, the Indian Muslim reformer, and Jamāluddīn Afghānī, the advocate of Pan-Islām, was essentially about whether reform of necessity involves secularization.[123] It is perhaps important to note that much of Afghānī and Muhammed 'Abduh's work in the context of the Middle East took place against the background of a secularizing programme emerging within the then Ottoman Empire. Farāh Antūn, a Christian friend but also intellectual opponent of 'Abduh, represented the secularizing Ottomanist view but, according to Cragg, failed to reckon with the inherent preoccupation with questions of power so characteristic of Islamic thought in this and other contexts.[124]

Nationalism was avowedly modernist in its intention and western in its inspiration, whether that was liberal or socialist. It has always been opposed by traditional Muslims as being contrary to the unity of the whole

---

123   See further Ruthven, *A Fury for God*, p. 66; and *The Cambridge History of Islam*, Vol. 2A, pp. 81ff.
124   Cragg, *The Arab Christian*, p. 156ff.

Umma. Nationalist leaders like Jinnah, Ataturk and Nasser were seen by such Muslims as the bearers of an alien ideology. Their ideas and policies were increasingly seen as the relics of a passing colonial era. In their place, Islamists began to argue for an ideology and a policy which was thoroughly Islamic. Islām, to them, was not just a matter of belief and ritual. It was *dīn*, a code which affected every area of human life: personal, social, economic and political. All Islamist rhetoric, whether Sunnīor Shī'a, Qutbi, Maudūdīan, or Khomeini's, insists on this central claim. In a very real sense, the rejection of nationalism was the rejection of colonialism and all that it had inspired and spawned in the Islamic world.

Nor was it just the classical manifestations of a colonial mentality which were being rejected. Neo-colonialism and its adjuncts have also played a strange part in the emergence and development of Islamism. In the early 1950s, the nationalist and moderately socialist government in Iran of Prime Minister Muhammed Mossadegh was toppled, and the Shah reinstated, in a coup engineered by Britain and the USA. The reason was that the government had withdrawn important oil concessions from the Western powers. In the years that followed, the increasing paranoia of the imperial government, and megalomania of the Royal Family itself, meant that a burgeoning middle class was unable to express itself freely, and democratic institutions were left undeveloped. By the time free expression began to be allowed, it was too late. Most radical dissenters were exiled and the rump of the National Front (Mossadegh's party) was unable to rally the masses. This was the opportunity for Ayatollah Khomeini to mobilize his supporters, while still in exile himself. They were joined by many progressive, liberal and socialist elements with the aim of getting rid of the Shah. Once this aim had been achieved and the revolutionaries had come to power, Khomeini set about ruthlessly liquidating his erstwhile allies. He could now enforce his ideology of *wilāyat-i-faqīh* or polity in which the 'Ulemā held supreme power on behalf of the absent Imām who is, himself, a successor of the Prophet. Typically Shī'ī doctrine is thus given a very contemporary twist. By 1980, the Islamic Revolution was complete in all essentials. To this day the main issue in Iran turns on the relationship between the *Majlis*, or popularly elected Parliament, and the so-called *Nigāhdārān* or Guardians. The latter evaluate all legislation in the light of the Shar'īa and can block any which seems to them un-Islamic. As was shown recently, they can also block parliamentary and presidential candidates from standing if their orthodoxy is suspect. As the Bible says, those who sow the wind, shall reap the whirlwind (Hos. 8:7): the destabilizing of a fragile democratic order led, eventually, to the horror of the full-scale revolution and to the establishment of a theocracy ruled by the recently politicized 'Ulemā.

In Afghanistan, a dynamic of a somewhat different kind operated. Here the Soviet Army had invaded the country in support of a socialist regime which was pretty brutal but which, nevertheless, had instituted some important reforms like the emancipation of women, compulsory education and various social justice measures. It had, however, alienated a largely conservative population which had risen up against it. The call for an international Jihād against the infidel came from a number of trans-national Muslim organizations who were able to raise funds from Muslim countries and individuals, as well as to recruit mujāhidīn from across the Islamic world to fight in Afghanistan. The Afghans still bore the brunt of the fighting, but their factionalism certainly did not help their cause. The large numbers of refugees in Pakistan's North-Western Frontier Province meant that the area became a base for operations. The West, already worried by events in Iran, saw this Soviet encroachment only in traditional cold war terms. It determined that Afghanistan would be the 'Vietnam' of the Soviet Union and began to arm, finance and train the various mujāhidīn groups with active assistance from Pakistan. The most sophisticated arms were supplied by the western powers. The heat-seeking 'Stinger' missile, for instance, which hitherto had only featured in government-to-government transactions was made available to those waging the Jihād.

The large numbers of refugees in Pakistan began to be radicalized. Funds from Pakistan, the Arabs and the West were made available disproportionately to the overtly Islamist groups. The male children of the refugees were recruited for the Madrassas (or traditional Islamic schools), where they were educated with the sons of Pakistan's teeming poor. As is well known now, it was in this pressure-cooker that the Tālibān (or students) were to be born. The overall effect of the whole adventure was that the West actively assisted in the emergence of an internationally linked Islamist movement which has become a threat not only to the liberty and stability of many in the Muslim world, but to the West itself. As with Iran, so here, the wind that was sown in the 1980s in Afghanistan and Pakistan has produced the whirlwind, not only of escalating violence in the Middle East and South Asia but also of the horrific events of '9/11' and their continuing consequences in Madrid, London and other parts of Europe.[125]

---

125   Ruthven, *A Fury for God*, pp. 169ff; and Kepel, *Jihād*, pp. 136ff.

We have seen already how intractable is the question of the land in the Palestinian–Israeli conflict. Whether we like it or not, much Arab opinion regards the State of Israel as an extension of western colonialism, if not of the crusades. The failure to negotiate in time with the Palestine Liberation Organisation, with its nationalist agenda, and covert Israeli patronage of the spiritual forebears of Hamās, has resulted in the gradual Islamization of the Palestine agenda both within and outside of the Holy Land. Christian and secular nationalists have been marginalized and the rhetoric has become more and more 'Jihādist', rather than of a kind which appeals to common principles of justice and compassion.[126]

Many other examples can be given from Egypt, the Sudan and North Africa where disillusionment with nationalism in the aftermath of imperialism and colonialism, or outrage at some neo-colonialist interventions, real or imagined, have been the triggers for Islamism of one kind or another.

PROGRESSIVE OR ISLAMIST: CRITIQUES OF CORRUPTION

I have noted elsewhere that the distinction between 'Islamist' and 'progressive' Muslim thought is not as clear-cut as some people may imagine. Thus the great Muslim reformers of the nineteenth and twentieth centuries, Jamāluddin Afghānī and Muhammad 'Abduh, for example, have an appeal both for 'progressives' and 'Islamists'. Rashīd Ridā who became a mentor of the *Ikhwān*, or Muslim

---

126 Kepel, *Jihād*, pp. 150ff; Ateek, *Justice and only Justice* (as note 54), pp. 115ff.

Brothers, had been a disciple of 'Abduh. 'Allāma Iqbāl, on the other hand, who is regarded as a 'progressive' on questions like the Sharī'a and relations with people of other faiths, is an admirer of that conservative reformer of the sixteenth century, Shaikh Ahmad Sirhindī.[127]

Both 'progressive' and 'Islamist', 'conservative' or 'liberal' reformers, however, have seen the roots of conflict, poverty and backwardness in the corruption of the ruling elite, secular and religious. Although Afghānī was a tireless campaigner against British imperialism, and had been exiled to India for this, he also recognized the un-Islamic nature of the despotism then current in many Muslim countries. He wanted the introduction of constitutional government and the guaranteeing of fundamental freedoms by both the colonial powers and local rulers. In his concern for reciprocity of obligations between ruler and ruled, he reflects the thought of the arch-conservative, Ibn Taimiyya.

Because of their perception of Islām as essentially egalitarian, many of the Muslim reformers flirted with socialism. Afghānī himself uses the term *ishtirākiyya*, by which he means a right sharing of wealth as taught and practised by the Prophet of Islām and his closest companions, and not the materialistic socialism then being propagated in Europe. Both Iqbāl and 'Ubaidullah Sindhi (d. 1944) had more than a sneaking sympathy for communist aspirations, even if they deplored its materialistic presuppositions. If only the communists had based their ideology on the prophetic concern for justice and not dialectical materialism! It is in this context that Iqbāl's remarks about Bolshevism plus God equalling Islām are to be judged – what was lacking in

---

127   Nazir-Ali, *Islam* (as note 14), pp. 102ff; Rahmān, *Revival and Reform*, pp. 166ff; and Iqbāl, *The Reconstruction of Religious Thought* (as note 98), pp. 193ff.

communism was the 'God dimension'. In his Persian work, the *Javēd-Nāmeh*, where a pilgrim is escorted through the heavens by Maulānā Jalāluddīn Rūmī, Iqbāl has Afghānī putting into words the charter of Islamic egalitarianism: it is to be a world without distinction of blood or colour, a world free of the difference between ruler and ruled.[128] In an Urdū poem he goes even further:

> It is time for people-power,
> Erase the old order wherever you see it!
> The field which does not provide a living for the peasant
> Set on fire every ear of corn in it![129]

Such sentiments were echoed and developed by poets, like Faiz Ahmed Faiz, who were explicitly committed to socialist programmes, if not to the philosophy of socialism as such. Islamists too, of various kinds, differentiate between the oppressor (*Zālim*) and the oppressed (*Mustad'afīn*). Khomeini made much of the latter term in his rallying speeches where he was trying to broaden his base. Both bazaar merchants deprived of their profits because of the Shah's policies, and Tehran slum-dwellers, were included in this term. The Shah and his secret police, Savak, were, of course, the oppressors or the 'arrogant ones' (*Mustakabirīn*). Militant groups in Egypt, Pakistan and North Africa employ similar criticism of corrupt governments whose Islām is at best suspect, and who oppress those who are struggling for a purely Islamic dispensation. In short, the perception that the ruling classes are corrupt, greedy and

---

128   M. Iqbal, *Javēd-Nāmeh*, Ghulam Ali, Lahore, 1974, p. 67.
129   M. Iqbal, *Bāl-i-Jibra'il* in *Kulliyāt-i-Iqbāl*, Ghulam Ali, Lahore, 1973, p. 110.

selfish fuels both the imagination and the rhetoric of most Islamist groups, whether Shī'a or Sunnī.[130] In this, they often claim to be the true successors of Islamic reformers down the years. One feature of this perception, which is significant for the international situation, is that these corrupt elites are hopelessly compromised with the West so that they can maintain their extravagant life-style, their international travel, their drinking of alcohol, gambling, illicit sex and the consumption of forbidden foods. The battle then against the 'satanic' West can begin with resistance to the corrupt elites of Muslim countries themselves.

THE REJECTION OF COMMAND ECONOMY SOCIALISM AND CAPITALISM

Politically centralizing tendencies throughout the nineteenth and twentieth centuries, which gave countries like Egypt, for instance, their present character and prominence, also resulted in the greater integration and central direction of economic life. Where reformers had created a sympathy for socialism, whether Marxist or Fabian, attempts were made to regulate economic life so that monopolies could be broken up or their creation prevented, to ensure a better distribution of wealth and income and to prevent the exploitation of labour. In some cases the distinct philosophy of 'Islamic Socialism' was developed and promoted. Its characteristic features include the permissibility of private property, though the extent of this can be disputed; competition is also allowed, but it must be strictly regulated according to Islamic principles; and class

---

130   Ruthven, *A Fury for God*, pp. 115f; Kepel, *Jihād*, pp. 111f.

war is rejected in favour of equality of opportunity and in terms of access to justice. Islamic socialism favours a fairer distribution of wealth and of income, but through fiscal means. Many of those who have espoused this kind of socialism have sought to integrate economic thinking with their view of the Umma as polity and with *dīn* (that is, with those religious and legal principles which undergird the whole life of the Umma).[131]

Some socialist-inspired regimes have, however, gone beyond such measures and have attempted to introduce 'command economy' models with high levels of centralized planning, control of the means of production and strict regulation of wages. At different times and in different ways such forms of socialism have been attempted in Syria, Egypt, Algeria, Southern Yemen and, partially, in Pakistan. They came to be characterized by erratic production, shoddy goods, high unemployment and featureless urban development. All of this led to *ennui* among the young and to the espousal of radical causes. In this system the rich were sometimes reduced to poverty, though often they escaped it, and the poor generally remained poor. Unbridled capitalism, however, which has had leases of life in countries like Pakistan (under Ayub Khan), Iran (under the Shah) and Indonesia (under Suharto), has resulted in large monopolies, gross distortions in the distribution of wealth and income, fiscal laxity, and labour has been mercilessly exploited. Not surprisingly, this has created widespread alienation, especially among the young and the urban poor. It is notorious that in Iran, the Islamic Revolution was fuelled by the alliance between the urban poor and the

---

131   Nazir-Ali, *Islam*, pp. 117ff; and H. Mintjes, *Al-Mushir*, Christian Study Centre, Rawalpindi, 1978, Nos 1, 2 and 4.

traditional merchant class who were losing their share of the nation's wealth to the *nouveaux riches* created by the imperial family on the back of oil exports and arms imports. It is no surprise, then, to be told that the Revolution moved from the slums of south Tehran to take control of the avenues and boulevards of north Tehran, where the Shah had been trying to build a replica of Switzerland, and which were out of bounds to the masses.[132] Gross and visible inequality has certainly been one of the causes in the prospering of Islamism: the poor, and especially the young among them, have felt that only the strict enforcement of the Sharī'a and governance according to Islamic principles could control the rampant greed of the rich and protect the poor from economic and social exploitation.

WHAT IS THE FUTURE OF ISLAMISM?

While it can be shown that the rejection of secular forms of nationalism and the adoption of various forms of Islamism have mostly taken root among the displaced and alienated urban and rural poor, and among their progeny who have acquired a certain amount of education, it has been supported and financed, in many cases, by rich, conservative states in the Arabian Peninsula and elsewhere. These states have often promoted a conservative form of Islām, within their own borders, to maintain the *status quo* and thus the privileges of the ruling classes, and also precisely to keep in check the kinds of movements they encourage

---

132   Kepel, *Jihād*, pp. 106ff. On the economic background to the revolution in Iran see Robert E. Looney, *Economic Origins of the Iranian Revolution*, Pergamon Press, New York, 1982.

elsewhere in the world. Osama bin Laden, then, the scion of a wealthy family from a wealthy country, leading the impoverished Tālibān, is but a picture of something which has been happening on a much wider scale for the last thirty years or so. The paradox is that what maintains a privileged *status quo* in one place becomes the instrument of revolution in another!

Some commentators have begun to observe a decline in the fortunes of Islamism. They have attributed this to the fragmentation of Islamist movements and the conflicts caused by the splitting and re-splitting. While some of the movements have paid lip-service to democracy, in fact there has been a deficit in the democratic agenda which has particularly alienated the young. In a number of countries, the Islamists are losing the attention of the young, who now have access to satellite television, the internet and mobile telephones. They can not only receive information from different parts of the world but they have the capacity to process it, compare the ideas and proposals they receive and, in due course, propagate them among their peers and beyond.[133] A leading Iranian Ayatollah confessed to me that the movement had 'lost the young', and this can be confirmed in a number of ways. Nor can the impact of 9/11 and the subsequent conflicts in Afghanistan and Iraq be underestimated. Directly or indirectly, they have led to the so-called 'turnaround' in Pakistan, and to demonstrations for greater popular participation in affairs of state in Lebanon, Syria and Egypt. The situation in the Holy Land has also been affected.

In some cases, Islamism is giving way to pragmatism. This is the case in Indonesia and, to some extent, in

---

133   Kepel, *Jihād*, pp. 361ff.

post-Mahathir Malaysia. In Pakistan, President Musharraf is promoting his views on 'enlightened moderation'. This involves a greater sense of restraint, as well as of openness to the rest of the world, on the part of Muslim nations; but it also appeals to non-Muslim countries to assist in the Muslim world in terms of education, exchange of information and people, and development. In both Egypt and Turkey, previously Islamist movements have reinvented themselves as 'moderates'. Most importantly, many Islamist leaders now see the need to distance themselves from violence of any kind and are committing themselves to the strengthening of civil society, the addressing of women's and minority issues, and to a fresh consideration of the role of religion in society.

This 'decline' in extremist rhetoric should not, however, be seen as the demise of militant Islamism. There are still significant 'flashpoints' in the world which can re-ignite militant fervour and this can lead to conflict and violence. The Holy Land is clearly an example of this: any confrontation in the Temple Mount area or the Old City of Jerusalem, in the Occupied Territories, or in Israel itself, can trigger conflict not only in Israel/Palestine but throughout the world. Kashmir, similarly, remains a thorn in the side of peace in South Asia. No Pakistani government can wholly contain militant movements within its borders as long as Kashmir is an issue. There will always be popular appeal for those who wish to train and even arm young people in Azad Kashmir and beyond for the liberation of Kashmir. If Pakistan and India truly want to check militancy in the area, a rapid and just solution of this problem is essential. No previously held dogmas, on either side, should be allowed to prevent a settlement, and if necessary international facilitation should be considered.

The tragedy of the recent earthquake in the area has elicited greater cooperation between traditional rivals. This could well be turned into an opportunity for peace. It is good that some work is being done in this respect.

It is understandable that Russia wishes to secure its southern flank but, once again, it needs to demonstrate to the international community that it is seeking only to put an end to militancy and is interested in recognizing the status and freedoms of the people of its predominantly Muslim republics and autonomous areas.

If there is to be a new order in the twenty-first century, we will need to come to a fresh understanding of the role of religion in state and society. We shall have to consider how cultures relate to spirituality and organized religion. We need to look at the relationship between religion and law and also how religion relates to conflict. It is important to give some attention to the conversations between faiths on questions of fundamental freedoms and how faith communities can participate in, or even lead in, matters of human development. In the following chapters we shall tackle some of these issues.

5

Some Issues in Dialogue Today I: Religion, Democracy and the State

We have seen how the long history of Christian, Muslim and Jewish encounter can be regarded as one of intermittent conflict along with periods of tolerance. It can also, however, be evaluated in terms of conversation and co-operation. Those who engaged in dialogue during the 'classical' period of Islamic ascendancy were attempting mainly to give an account of their faith and, if possible, to show it in the most favourable light. The exchanges between the Sūfīs and the Christian monastic tradition were about the nature of mystical experience, the kinds of ascetic discipline necessary for a mystical life and, most importantly, the figure of Jesus as an exemplar of the wholly devoted mystic and ascetic.[134] Christian translators and scholars contributed to the conversation through their work in a number of distinctive ways.[135]

---

134   See further Iqbāl, *The Development of Metaphysics in Persia* (as note 15), pp. 76ff; Hasan Dehqani-Tafti, *Christ and Christianity Amongst the Iranians*, Vols I–III, Sohrab Books, Basingstoke, 1992; and Tarif Khalidi, *The Muslim Jesus*, Harvard University Press, Cambridge, MA, 2001.
135   Nazir-Ali, *Islam* (as note 14), pp. 70ff.

WHAT IS DIALOGUE?

In the New Testament period, the terms *dialegomai* and *dialogizomai* can be thought of as meaning 'arguments for the sake of reaching the truth'. This sense of a dialectical process which would lead the interlocutor to acknowledge Christian truth remained throughout the Patristic period. It can be seen early on in the dialogical methods of Justin Martyr and later in the dialogues of St John of Damascus with Muslims already mentioned. Indeed, we may say that such an understanding of dialogue remained dominant until modern times. Muslims also, following Qur'ānic injunction (3:64), have a tradition of discussion, especially with the People of the Book. This also has, traditionally, been regarded as establishing the truth of Islamic revelation. There is a wealth of writing which engages in such discussion with Christians and Jews.[136]

How do we move on from here? We may say straight away that the older practice of providing information about our faith to our partner in dialogue retains its value. It is not necessarily polemical or even apologetic in nature, and it can provide us with valuable information about what people believe and how this motivates their behaviour. Professor Eric Sharpe has called this kind of dialogue 'discursive'. Following the monks and the Sūfīs, we may say that conversation about spiritual experience can also be illuminating and mutually beneficial. Sharpe calls this 'interior' dialogue. There is then the dialogue which leads

---

136 See further Nazir-Ali, *Mission and Dialogue* (as note 48), pp. 75ff; and *Citizens and Exiles* (as note 6), pp. 115ff. See also Jean-Marie Gaudeul, *Encounters and Clashes: Islam and Christianity in History*, Vols I and II, Pontifical Institute for Islamic Studies, Rome, 1984.

to the identification of those values which are necessary for living together and building up the community. These may have to do with the importance of family life, the treatment of the vulnerable, access to public services for all, and equal opportunity. Even if arising from different points of view, the upholding of the dignity and worth of all human beings, and the care of the world in which we live, will be central in such a dialogue. In today's world, it is increasingly important that there should be dialogue between people of different faiths on matters having to do with fundamental freedoms. These will certainly include the relationship between freedom of expression and public order, freedom of worship and of religious belief generally (including the possibility of changing one's belief), and freedom of movement without undue restrictions for people on the basis of their religion, race or national origin. The position of groups such as women or religious and ethnic minorities must also be a matter of dialogue.[137]

The Vatican has identified the dialogue of *life* which takes place among neighbours, friends or workmates. The dialogue of *scholars* explores, at a theological level, some of the issues just mentioned. I have been privileged to have been part of such a process from its inception in the wake of '9/11' and with the encouragement of the Prime Minister and successive Archbishops of Canterbury. From considering the background to that tragedy and a common study of the Bible and the Qur'ān, we are now considering how the view of religious communities as distinctive societies affects their relationship with wider society,

---

137 Eric Sharpe, 'The Goals of Inter-Religious Dialogue', in John Hick (ed.), *Truth and Dialogue: The Relationship Between World Religions*, Sheldon, London, 1974, pp. 77ff.

nationally and internationally. There is also formal dialogue between representative institutions such as the one between Al-Azhar As-Sharif, the premier Sunī place of learning, and the Anglican Communion (which I lead on the Anglican side). The Roman Catholic Church has a similar and concurrent dialogue. Having considered the nature of dialogue, the kinds there may be and some approaches to dialogue, what are the burning issues which come up in dialogue today? Naturally, to a certain extent, the identification of these will depend on individual experience but I will outline a few which may have resonances with the experiences of others.[138]

THE RELATIONSHIP BETWEEN RELIGION AND THE STATE: CHRISTIAN AND MUSLIM PERSPECTIVES

A ubiquitous theme these days is that of the relationship between religion and the state. Since the Peace of Westphalia (1648) the paradigm which has persisted, in Western Europe and North America at least, has been that of the practical separation of religion from the affairs of the state, especially in the formation and development of policy, whether domestic or foreign. The background to this consensus is the formative role which religion is thought to have played in the various conflicts preceding the Peace,

---

138 See further *Dialogue and Proclamation, The Bulletin*, Pontifical Council for Inter-Religious Dialogue, Rome, May 1991; M. Ipgrave (ed.), *The Road Ahead: A Christian–Muslim Dialogue*, Church House Publications, London, 2002; and M. Ipgrave (ed.), *Scriptures in Dialogue*, Church House Publications, London, 2004.

even though it is nowadays generally admitted that it was by no means the only factor in many of these conflicts.[139]

A result of removing the 'sacred canopy' from affairs of the State has been to empty and strip the public square of values grounded in faith, leaving only formal rules of engagement, a residual but fading sense of public morality, or attempts to introduce values (sometimes religiously-based ones) covertly. An increasing spiritual and moral vacuum is experienced by many in the West, and a question which must arise in the minds of at least the thoughtful is: with what and how and when will the vacuum be filled? There are a number of answers to this question, not all of them desirable.[140] In such a context, it may be worthwhile to consider various Christian and Muslim attitudes to the State.

BIBLICAL ATTITUDES TO THE STATE

The origins of Christian attitudes to the State are to be found in the Bible. Already in ancient Israel, the emergence of the monarchy was reluctantly recognized as necessary (maybe even as a necessary evil) and the rights and duties of kingship were prescribed (1 Sam. 8–10). The stories about Nathan and David (2 Sam. 12) and Elijah and Ahab (1 Kgs 21) show us that the monarchy was not regarded as absolute but as accountable to the laws of God. During their

---

139 See further Scott M. Thomas, 'Taking Religious and Cultural Pluralism Seriously', in Petito and Hatzopoulos (eds), *Religion in International Relations* (as note 9), pp. 22ff.

140 O. O'Donovan, *The Desire of the Nations*, CUP, Cambridge, 1996; also his submission to the Evangelical Alliance's Commission of Inquiry on Faith and Nation, 2004 (as note 30).

period of exile in Babylon, the Jewish people were told to work for and pray for the well-being of the place to which they had been exiled (Jer. 29:7). The general situation in the older Testament, with regard to foreign rulers, is to respect them and even serve them, provided that such respect and service do not in any way compromise the duty and worship owed to God alone (this position is worked out, in a sustained way, in the Book of Daniel, for example). With Cyrus the Persian, however, there is already a development, in that he is regarded as the Lord's anointed in the fulfilment of the divine plan for the return of the exiles from Babylon (Isa. 45:1f.).

At the time of Jesus, the Jewish people paid taxes to the Roman and other authorities. The *censum* or poll-tax, which was universally hated but nevertheless paid, and the taxes levied by the Herodian rulers are examples of such payment. In the context of the *censum*, Jesus' teaching about rendering to Caesar what is his and to God what properly belongs to God (Mk 12:13–17 and parallels) indicates the scope of obedience to temporal rulers. There is an obligation to pay for the protection and the amenities provided, but in such a way and to such an extent that the rights of God are not usurped and divine sovereignty is not compromised.[141] It seems that after the destruction of the Temple in AD 70, the tax for the upkeep of the Temple was transferred to the Roman authorities who used it for the cult of Jupiter. The continued payment of this tax exempted the Jews from active participation in the imperial cult but required, to some extent, an implicit recognition of it. It

---

141   See further C. E. B. Cranfield, *The Gospel According to St Mark*, CUP, Cambridge, 1966, pp. 371ff; also, Alan Storkey, *Jesus and Politics: Confronting the Powers*, Baker, Grand Rapids, MI, 2005, pp. 211ff.

seems that at least some Christians wanted to continue belonging to the Synagogue precisely so that they could pay the tax and thus avoid ascribing divine honours to the emperor. Their expulsion from the synagogues at the same time as Domitian's demand that he should be worshipped as *dominus et deus* exposed them to the particular persecution which is referred to in the Apocalypse of St John.[142]

Before the full force of the Neronian persecution was felt by the Christians, Paul's experience of the *Pax Romana* led him to the positive view of imperial power which we find in Romans 13. God is the fount of all authority and the authority of earthly rulers is derived from God. Human government is an aspect of the divine ordering of creation and is necessary for the common good. It is appropriate, therefore, for Christians to obey the laws of the State, to pay all taxes due to them and to give proper respect to the authorities.

The principles enunciated in a time of peace held, however, even on the eve of and during a fiery persecution. The First Letter of Peter, which was probably written even as the persecution of Nero was breaking out, echoes much of what is found in St Paul's Letter to the Romans. There are admittedly some differences which arise perhaps from the context: the emphasis now is not on the divine ordering of societies, but on the various human forms in which such ordering is expressed. Christians are told, nevertheless, to submit to 'every human institution' which exists to promote human welfare and the punishment of those who would harm it (1 Pet. 2:13–17).

There is always, however, a *caveat* first expressed by Peter

---

142   See Colin Hemer, 'The Letters to the Seven Churches of Asia in their Local Setting', *Journal for the Study of the New Testament* 11 (1986), 7ff.

and the other apostles at the very beginning in their confrontation with the Jewish authorities: that they must obey God rather than human beings (Acts 5:29). Human authorities are to be obeyed as long as they act in accordance with their mandate and do not trespass on what is God's will for his creation. If they do, for example by restricting people's freedom to respond to the love of God in confession of belief and worship, they are to be resisted. 'Caesar' can certainly transgress the limits of his jurisdiction by claiming divine honours and by waging war against the saints. St Paul could see this happening if the restraining hand of the law was withdrawn (2 Thess. 2:6f.); and for Augustine, if justice is removed, the State simply becomes a system of legalized robbery.[143] The idea that rulers are subject to the law of God and not above it has had important consequences in constitutional history and in making rulers subject to the law which gives them authority to govern but also protects those who are governed.[144]

By the time of Domitian, the imperial cult had become so oppressive for Christians that the wise magistrate of the Letter to the Romans becomes the beast from the abyss who wages war on God's people in the last book of the Bible, the Revelation of St John the Divine (Rev. 13). During the second and third centuries, there were periods of peace for the Church but also periods of violent persecution. During this time, Christians developed ways of explaining their faith to the pagan world around them, especially to those in authority and to demand justice from them. They were also keen to assure their rulers that they prayed for them

---

143 Augustine, *The City of God* (Library of Nicene and Post-Nicene Fathers), T&T Clark, Edinburgh, 1993, 4:4, p. 66.
144 Storkey, *Jesus and Politics*, pp. 184f.

regularly as, of course, we do today. (Walter Wink and Lesslie Newbigin remind us that the victory over the imperial system was not won by seizing the levers of power. It was won when those about to be martyred knelt down and prayed for the emperor.)[145] The 'Apology' became a favourite form of doing these things and, although it was often addressed to those who wielded political and military power, it was sometimes more general.[146]

Much is known about the persecution of Christians throughout the Roman Empire but there was persecution elsewhere as well, especially within the domains of the other superpower of the time, the Empire of Persia. The fifth-century Greek historian, Sozomen, writing about the persecutions of the previous century in the Persian Empire, tells us that there were at least sixteen thousand martyrs. He is well aware that there may well have been others.[147]

THE EDICTS OF TOLERATION

The edicts of toleration, when they came in the two Empires, had somewhat different results. The edicts of Yazdgard in 410 recognized the Christians as a valid community in the land. Its affairs were organized on the basis of the now well-known *millet* system which survived into Islamic times and was used by the Ottomans right up to the modern period. As a *millet*, Christians had rights and obligations in relation to the Empire but they remained a

---

145 Newbigin, *The Gospel in a Pluralist Society* (as note 28), p. 210. See also Walter Wink, *Naming the Powers: Language of Power in the New Testament*, Fortress Press, Augsburg, MN, 1985.

146 See further Sider, *The Gospel and its Proclamation* (as note 68).

147 Young, *Patriarch, Shah and Caliph* (as note 92), pp. 21ff.

distinct community within it. The Edict of Milan, on the other hand, a century earlier, led eventually to the emergence of the *Corpus Christianum*, the idea that, while Church and State were distinct societies, they were united in one commonwealth and manifested different aspects of it. In Byzantium, the Emperor became the dominant partner in this alliance, whereas in the West the Middle Ages were marked by claims of the Papacy to be dominant.[148] The Persian and Roman models offer two perspectives on being Church vis à vis the State. In the former, Christians are a distinct but tolerated community who are able to make a limited contribution to the Empire in which they are set. In the latter, there is virtual identification between Empire and Church. In the course of history, the Byzantine model of the godly king or emperor who had jurisdiction in both Church and State became more and more attractive to emerging monarchies in Western Europe and is at the basis of the various settlements which were concluded at the time of the Reformation.[149]

The Eastern and Western parts of the Roman Empire are not, of course, the only examples of the *Corpus Christianum*: already towards the end of the third century the nation of Armenia had become the first to be officially Christian, and Ethiopia became a Christian Empire during the fifth century at the latest. By contrast, some churches, like the Coptic Orthodox and the Syrian Jacobites have nearly always existed as distinct communities within polities which have often been hostile to them. In India, the rulers

---

148   On this see Jaroslav Pelikan, *The Excellent Empire: The Fall of Rome and the Triumph of the Church*, Harper and Row, San Francisco, 1987; and George Every, *The Byzantine Patriarchate*, SPCK, London, 1947.

149   See further Chadwick, *The Reformation* (as note 37).

were not always hostile but the ancient churches there were always a clear minority.

TRADITIONS OF DISSENT

Throughout the story of the Church there have been groups of Christians, such as the Lollards, the Hussites and the Waldensians, who have emphasized the nature of the Church as a distinct and gathered community which does not need the arm of civil authority to give it special protection, and which cannot be identified with natural groupings, whether ethnic or territorial. The Reformation period gave such groups great encouragement, so that some emerged from the shadows and new ones came into existence. Although they differed markedly from one another and were not free of conflict even within themselves, they were characterized by a certain family resemblance. They believed in the pure congregation, or society of saints, who were called out of the world and maintained a distinctive life-style which often included refusal of military service, pacifism, and extreme simplicity. They rejected both the worldliness of contemporary Roman Catholicism and the Erastianism of the 'mainstream' Reformation churches. Because of this, they were sometimes persecuted on all sides.[150]

Even within the so-called mainstream, however, there were groups who wanted their church to be more like the New Testament churches and, therefore, less aligned to the State, however 'Christian' it claimed to be. There were others who had serious reservations about the Erastian aspect of Church–State relations in many parts of Europe,

---

150   Chadwick, *The Reformation*, pp. 14f, 188ff.

and yet others who could see that the divided state of the Christian churches would remain unless the link with the State was somehow loosened. The Puritans in the Church of England, for example, wanted the Reformation to continue and were determined to resist the monarch and the bishops in this matter. Their legacy remains an important one in the Anglican Communion today. The Non-Jurors emerged as a party which resisted the King because they believed in the divine right of monarchs. Having taken the Oath of Allegiance to the exiled James II, they refused to take one to the newly-arrived William and Mary. They included the Archbishop of Canterbury, eight other bishops and four hundred clergy. The Non-Jurors were active in liturgical development, in ecumenism (especially in relation to the Orthodox), and in the fostering of spirituality. For our purposes, however, their most important characteristic was a high conception of the Church as a spiritual society with its own laws, which was held alongside an equally high view of the monarchy and of the obedience due to it.

It was this principle which they bequeathed to the Tractarians and which was at stake in the attempt by the Whig government in the 1830s to suppress a number of bishoprics in Ireland. The question was not whether they ought to be suppressed, but whether the government should be acting in a matter which was proper to the Church. John Keble's sermon on 'National Apostasy' in 1833 tackled this issue, and is generally regarded as the beginning of the Catholic revival in the Church of England.[151] This revival initiated

---

151   See further M. Nazir-Ali, 'The Vocation of Anglicanism', *Anvil* 6 (2), 1989, 113ff; and *From Everywhere to Everywhere: A World View of Christian Mission*, Collins, London, 1990, pp. 46ff.

fresh ways of thinking about the relationship between Church and State.

David Nicholls has discerned two main tendencies in Anglican Catholic thought: the incarnationalist and the redemptionist. The incarnationalist approach he regards as optimistic and gradualist: the Kingdom of God comes slowly, silently and peacefully; as the mighty are lowered from their seats, this is so gently done that they do not feel the bump when they hit the ground! Against this tendency are the redemptionists. Although they too regard the Incarnation as important, they also emphasize the Cross where there is a decisive battle between good and evil. Whilst creation, for them, is fundamentally good, they take due account of the pervasive effects of the Fall, particularly on the social, economic and political structures of human society. Whilst they are prepared to work with these, they refuse to sacralize them and, most importantly, to confuse the Church with them. Both Nicholls and Dr Rowan Williams, now Archbishop of Canterbury, refer in this respect to the work of John Neville Figgis. Figgis regarded the state as an 'association of associations', but an association which had the power to balance the claims and order the relations of its constitutive parts. Within such a structure, the Church can maintain its distinct witness to the Gospel which continually challenges the foundations on which the kingdoms of this world are built. It is interesting, in this connection, to note that Dr Williams refers to Figgis in the context of the need to take liberation theologies seriously – theologies which, at the very least, oblige us to analyse patterns of domination and deprivation as obstacles to the transformation offered by the Gospel. A theological critique of our social and political context implies a Christian community which has an understanding of distinctiveness, as well as of belonging, in the situation in which it finds itself.

Both Williams and Nicholls are aware of the questions raised by Figgis' work: the extent to which societies are providentially ordered for the sake of the common good, for instance; and also the basis for Christian cooperation with the secular organs of the State in matters of justice, compassion and access.[152]

Such views of Church–State relationships leave little room for coercion on either side: the State must respect the proper autonomy of the Church, except where the liberty and welfare of others may be involved; and the Church must, as Figgis urged, recognize a proper sphere for the State to govern. What else can we say of this relationship? There can be what Nicholls somewhat dismissively calls 'the influencing of society'. This is hardly revolutionary and certainly melioristic but often effective, nevertheless. There can also be 'prophetic witness' over and against society, towards which Nicholls would be more sympathetic; and there can be 'struggle' on behalf of those who are powerless, excluded and deprived. It is, of course, possible to imagine not only the influencing of society, but also prophetic witness, and even struggle, taking place both outside and within the councils of State, if the Church is afforded a voice there.

---

152   R. Williams and D. Nicholls, *Politics and Theological Identity: Two Anglican Essays*, Jubilee, London, 1984, pp. 21ff and pp. 33ff.

COERCION, INFLUENCE OR PROPHETIC STRUGGLE?

Even where there is a formal separation of Church and State, however, we find that forms of government and structures of State can be formatively influenced by a religious tradition. The American Declaration of Independence and the subsequent constitutional history of the USA amply bear this out.[153] In Europe and elsewhere, for example Armenia and Ethiopia as examples of 'old' Christendoms, the Philippines in Asia, and many states in today's Africa, there has been and continues to be a more direct link between Christianity and constitutional arrangements. Law, moreover, if it is to have moral and not merely coercive force, must be grounded in a spiritual and moral tradition on which it can also draw in the course of its development. No doubt there are analogues to these matters in the world of Islām which our Muslim friends will be able to discuss, but of course, as we shall see, a developmental view of the relation between Law and Religion cannot be just about the adoption of legal codes framed in a different age for very different purposes.

This brings me to questions of dialogue and reciprocity. We need to arrive at a point where we can frankly acknowledge not only the historical position of Islām or Christianity vis à vis constitutional and legal arrangements in various countries, but their influence *in the present* and *for the future*. Such an acknowledgement would deliver us from the false hopes associated with allegedly secular politics. We will still need to ask, however, in a dialogical context, how people of

---

153 On this debate see George Weigel, *The Cube and the Cathedral: Europe, America and Politics Without God*, Basic Books, New York, 2005.

other faiths, and of none, can creatively contribute in a social and political situation which has largely been formed under the influence of a particular tradition. We will also need to ensure that the commitment to freedoms of expression and of worship and to participation in political, economic and social life in one context is also expected in other contexts. Those engaged in dialogue have committed themselves to such basic freedoms and access to community life for all in every place, and particularly where they themselves have influence.

We know that St Paul used his Roman citizenship to good effect in the course of his missionary work (Acts 16:37–39, 22:25–29), whereas the first letter of St Peter describes Christians as strangers and exiles in this world (1 Pet. 1:1, 2:11). This tension between belonging and not-belonging, between being citizens and yet exiles in the present order, has remained in Christian thinking about the relationship between faith and nation, faith and ethnicity, and faith and culture. It is best summed up in a second- or third-century letter written to an enquirer, the so-called *Epistle to Diognetus*. The writer describes Christians in this way:

They dwell in their own countries but as strangers. They share all things as citizens and suffer all things as foreigners. Every foreign country is their home and their own country is foreign to them. They marry like everyone else and have children but they do not expose their offspring. They share their table with others but not the marriage bed. Their lot is to be in the flesh, yet they do not live according to the flesh. They pass their time on earth but their citizenship is in heaven. They obey the appointed laws but surpass them in their own lives. They love everyone but are persecuted by everyone. They are unknown and are condemned. They are put to death and gain life. Although they are poor, they make many rich. They have nothing and yet they have everything. They are dishonoured but are glorified in their dishonour. They are regarded as evil but are justified. They are abused but they bless. They are insulted and they honour. When they do good and are called evil, they rejoice as those receiving life.[154]

The tension cannot easily be resolved and we have to live with it creatively; both belonging and not-belonging, as part of society and yet strangers to some of its standards and values, as citizens but also as exiles.

By way of contrast, Islām is alleged to have a straightforward relationship with the State. Islamic Law is deemed to be supreme and the 'ulemā or religious scholars, who are its custodians and interpreters, claim a decisive place for themselves in constitutional, political, social and even economic matters. No law can be promulgated and no institution established which is contrary to the injunctions of the Qur'ān and the *Sunna* (or the practice of the Prophet of Islām). Both Muslim and non-Muslim scholars often assess the situation in this way and, until recently, it might well have been described as the 'reigning orthodoxy'.[155] But is

154   *Epistle to Diognetus*, The Apostolic Fathers, Vol. II, Loeb Classical Library, Harvard, 1913, 5:1–16, pp. 359f. Also Nazir-Ali, *Citizens and Exiles*.
155   On these matters, see Gai Eaton, *Islam and the Destiny of Man*, Islamic Texts, Cambridge, 1994, pp. 177ff. For an 'Islamist' view of the matter, forcefully expressed, see Maulānā Abu A'la Maudūdī's writings, especially *Haqīqat-ī-Jihād*, Taj, Lahore 1966; *Musalman Our Maujūda Siyāsi Kashmākash*, Maktaba Jamā'at-I-Islāmī, Pathankot, 1941–42; and *The Rights*

the situation really so simple and can it be so easily described?

A common thread running through both the post-Westphalian discussion in the West and in the context of Islamic polity is the assumption that the role of religion vis à vis the State must always be that of *coercion*. As we have seen, in the West, the background to this may be the over-weening claims by the medieval Papacy in relation to the emergent monarchs of Europe, or attempts by some elements, at the time of the Reformation, to establish theocratic or near-theocratic states. In Islām, it is sometimes the attempt by contemporary movements for reform and renewal to align themselves with a recurring tendency throughout Islamic history in yearning for a theocratic dispensation.[156]

While these backgrounds need to be acknowledged, we must also ask whether the evidence has to be read in this way? Is it still possible for Europe to recognize the formative influence of Christianity on its institutions, laws and values? In countries where there is an established Christian tradition, such as England or Scotland, what contribution can such traditions continue to make so that law and policy-making both have the spiritual and moral undergirding which is so necessary in establishing their legitimacy?

Where there has been a separation of the State from any

---

of *Non-Muslims in an Islamic State*, Lahore, 1961. For a rebuttal see M. Tahir Ahmad, *Murder in the Name of Allah*, Lutterworth, Cambridge, 1989. For Western views of the issues see Kenneth Cragg, *Am I not your Lord?*, Melisende, London, 2002, pp. 57ff; and Colin Chapman, *Islam and the West*, Carlisle, Paternoster, 1998, pp. 123ff.

156 *The Cambridge History of Islam* (as note 83), Vol. 1A, pp. 71ff; Rahmān, *Revival and Reform in Islam* (as note 118), pp. 132ff. For how these views affect non-Muslims, see Ye'or, *The Dhimmi* (as note 61), pp. 172ff, 194ff etc.

one ecclesial tradition, as in the United States, it may still be necessary to identify the spiritual influences on the Constitution and other fundamental documents, as well as to ask how such influence is brought to bear on law and policy-making today.[157]

In other words, it seems more sensible to speak of the relationship between religion and the State as one of *influence, prophetic witness and struggle* rather than coercion (it may even be possible to read at least some of history in this way). This would allow us to evaluate the influence exerted through established channels but also through popular movements of reform and protest. In the UK, the impact of early Methodism on the mobilization of workers; of the Salvation Army on the widespread recognition of temperance as a virtue (even if hard to recognize today!); and of the Clapham Sect on issues such as the abolition of the slave-trade and of slavery itself, the education of the poor, and working conditions in mines and factories; all point to the very diverse ways in which religious belief can affect cultural values and influence state policy.[158]

As 'establishment' has continued to modify (some might say attenuate) in Western Europe, churches like the Church of England and the Church of Scotland have sought more and more to exert influence, to give advice and express opinion. They have had to rely on the quality of their views, rather than the views being *theirs*, to obtain a respectful hearing. This has certainly meant the valuing of expertise in areas of public life and of rapid change, but it

---

157   See further Weigel, *The Cube and the Cathedral*; and Nazir-Ali, 'Thinking and Acting Morally' (as note 31).
158   A comprehensive account is given in Bebbington, *Evangelicalism in Modern Britain* (as note 13).

has also required the churches to hone their skills for the public arena. Although there is much to do, this has, in fact, assisted the public mission of the Church.

IS ISLAM A THEOCRACY?

Turning once again to Islām, the very early days of the *Khulafa Ar-Rāshidīn* (The Righteous Caliphs) may perhaps be described as a theocracy or a near-theocracy, though even then intermediate institutions were beginning to develop. The *Khārijites* (literally the ones who go out) rejected such developments. Their cry was *lā hukm illā lillahi* (no rule but that of God alone!). In adopting such a stance, they prefigured movements in Islām down to present times which have rejected any compromise or even dialogue with the secular world and have called for true believers to leave compromised and apostate Islām for the purity of their own organization. *Takfīr wa'l Hijra* (meaning the declaration of a society as unbelieving and making an exit from it) is only one such movement, but its name suggests the mind-set of a number.[159]

On the whole, however, historical Islamic polity cannot be characterized as a theocracy. The Caliphate itself developed as an intermediate institution, especially when it became hereditary and monarchical. The 'ulema and *fuqahā*, the scholars and the jurists, who had the important tasks of interpreting, codifying and implementing the Sharī'a, or divine law, in every area of life – political, social, economic, family and personal – naturally assumed great

---

159   Hitti, *History of the Arabs* (as note 71), p. 182; Kepel, *Jihād* (as note 121); and Ruthven, *A Fury for God* (as note 120).

importance; but so too, though in a different way, did the Sūfīs, the mystics of Islām, who became influential not only through their teaching but through the creation of movements of loyalty to them. These orders, as well as the shrines and the *khānqāhs* (or communities associated with them), have had a very important role in defining the nature of various Muslim societies, as well as being organs through which both support of and dissent from government policies could be voiced. Wherever they have been suppressed, as a matter of state policy, the political (not to speak of spiritual) conversation has been impoverished. As Spencer Trimingham has pointed out, the orders had a very important social, political and economic role. These orders came to be associated with different elements in society, and in this way they exerted influence on military, commercial and state matters.[160] Nor should we forget here the ways in which the numerous non-Muslim communities were organized within the Muslim world. As we have seen, from time to time and from place to place, they had a relatively high degree of autonomy in civil, commercial, religious and even judicial matters (especially in relation to personal and family law), even if they were also sometimes discriminated against and persecuted.[161]

---

160 Trimingham, *The Sufi Orders in Islam*; and Kepel, *Jihād* (as note 94), pp. 48ff.
161 See further Bat Ye'or, *Islam and Dhimmitude*, Associated University Press, New Jersey, 2002.

RELIGION AND DEMOCRACY

In any discussion of the relationship between religion and the state, the question about democracy arises sooner or later. How is democracy related to religion? Has it arisen from religious ideals or does it have different roots? How have religions responded to democracy in different parts of the world and what is the situation today?

In ancient Israel, the monarch was supposed to have been chosen by the people and his duties strictly prescribed (Deut. 17:14–20). Other leaders similarly are to be chosen by the people (Deut. 1:13), even if appointed by Moses. The leaders are to be characterized by qualities of humility, truth, honesty and wide knowledge. This tradition was continued by the Rabbis. The inherent and unique dignity of human persons is, according to Judaism, best protected and nurtured within a democratic framework. It is recognized, however, that Judaism has not always been faithful to this vision, not least in the ambiguity of democracy to be found in the State of Israel.[162]

It should be said, at once, that in this regard Christianity too has a mixed record: on the one hand, Christian ideas about the dignity of the human person, the necessity of personal faith, and the importance of individual responsibility have all contributed to the development of democratic ideas. The Reformation's recovery of these insights and their enhancement appears to have prepared the ground for popular movements, religious and secular, in the centuries which were to follow. Such insights could lead

---

162   See the successive articles by David Rosen, Irving Greenberg and Robert Ash in Alan Race and Ingrid Shafer (eds), *Religions in Dialogue: From theocracy to democracy*, Ashgate, Aldershot, 2002, pp. 23ff.

either to William Tyndale's 'Christian commonwealth', which united all Christians and in which all were of equal worth; or to the typically 'Anabaptist' solution of strictly separating the Christian community from the paraphernalia of the state. The latter led to a polity like the United States which was Christian but in which the State was quite separate and not to be identified with any one Church. The former led to the gradual emergence of constitutional monarchies in the United Kingdom and continental Europe.[163]

On the other hand, the doctrine of the divine right of kings, of *cujus regio ejus religio*, and the uniformity which these demand, prevented or at least retarded the emergence of democracy. The acknowledged desire by the Roman Catholic Church to impose conformity likewise led to the condemnation by that Church of democracy and other libertarian notions, as late as the 1864 *Syllabus Errorum* of Pius IX.[164]

The term democracy has meant different things – at different times. In the Greek *polis* it meant the exercise of the franchise by free men; women and slaves being excluded from both franchise and governance. In most Western countries, there were tests of property and the like before the vote could be cast, and women were given the vote, in historical terms, quite recently.

In discussing democracy, Christian writers often point out that for democracy to be just there is a need for adherence to some corporate values. As we have seen,

---

163 See further David Edwards, *Christian England*, Collins, London, 1988, pp. 240ff; Chadwick, *The Reformation*, pp. 188ff; and David Daniell in his edition of Tyndale's *The Obedience of a Christian Man*, Penguin, London, 2000, pp. xxvf.
164 Race and Shafer (eds), *Religions in Dialogue*, pp. 73ff.

others regard democracy as a way of balancing power among social groups and as a safeguard against tyranny. While aware of democracy's limitations, most Christians have seen the force of Reinhold Niebuhr's argument that democracy is not just about freedom and choice but about protection from oppression: 'Man's capacity for justice makes democracy possible; but man's inclination to injustice makes democracy necessary.' Such a view is consonant with a properly Christian anthropology which thinks of human beings as both destined for glory and able to sink to levels lower than the beasts of the field.[165]

As a matter of history, democracy has flourished in countries with a Christian background, especially where there has been resistance to totalitarian rule, whether ecclesiastical or civil, and where toleration of diverse religious opinions has emerged. It also seems to flourish in contexts like India where the dominant religious tradition has been deeply influenced, indeed transformed, by Christian ideas, whether through social reformers such as Raja Ram Mohan Roy, literary figures like Rabindranath Tagore, or statesmen like Mahatma Gandhi.[166] Countries like Japan and Korea are examples of situations where democracy has gone hand in hand with considerable economic and social westernization. In Africa, it is struggling to emerge in both 'liberal' contexts, such as South Africa, and those which retain a 'socialist' framework like Tanzania.

All of this raises the topical question about the relation of democracy to Islām. Are the two as antithetical as is sometimes claimed? We have seen that Islām need not be a

---

165   R. Niebuhr, *The Children of Light and the Children of Darkness*, Nisbet, London, 1945, p. vif.
166   See further M. M. Thomas, *The Acknowledged Christ of the Indian Renaissance*, SCM Press, London, 1969.

theocracy; but does that open the path for plural, democratic states within the Islamic world? What about the reserve which even courageous modernizers have about the term? It is certainly the case that in many quarters, the pressure for democracy is regarded as a thinly veiled attempt to perpetrate and perpetuate Western hegemony. Many of those who think of themselves as the moral and spiritual guardians of Islamic societies tend to regard democracy as leading to moral and spiritual laxity – which they also see as being the main causes of social dysfunction in the West.

Many Arab and Islamic countries use a variant of the word *jumhūrīya* in their formal title. This comes from the verb *jamhara*, and means to gather, collect or assemble. Is this something fundamental to societies in which Islām is dominant, or is it just an attempt to render the term 'republic' into acceptable Arabic? It may be more fruitful to examine the idea of the umma in Islām. This is a word derived from Hebrew and Aramaic, but is used specifically in the Qur'ān to refer to bodies of people within the divine providence. God has sent a messenger to each umma but, generally speaking, they have not been heeded (6:42, 10:47, etc.). Some, however, especially among the Jews and Christians, *have* heeded the messengers, and they are called umma in a particular sense (3:113, 5:69, etc.). The Qur'ān recognizes that a plurality of umam is an aspect of God's will (10:19, 11:118, 16:93, etc.). The term reaches full significance, however, after the *hijra* when the Prophet establishes the first 'Islamic' Umma. In this he goes beyond the community of Muslims, and includes within it those who were Jews, Christians, or even pagans, on conditions of honour and equality. Gradually, this constitution of the community of Medīna was replaced by an Umma that consisted only of Muslims. The question can be asked, however, whether those who aspire to establish Islamic states today wish to do so on the example and model of their Prophet himself; and if not, why not?[167]

The varied texture of the umma, and the fact that the Qur'ān recognizes different vocations for groups within it (e.g. 3:104), leads to the question of decision-making within it. It is here that the practice of *shūrā* becomes so important. The background to this is to be found in pre-Islamic tribal society in Arabia, where the Sheikh would consult the tribal elders. Their advice was not binding on him, and he could overrule it. In the Sūra itself called *As-shūrā*, the conduct of affairs in the community through mutual consultation is praised (42:38) and, later on, the Prophet himself is urged to take counsel with the community before he makes a decision (3:159). Some have held that such consultation could not bind the Prophet of Islām then, and should not bind the head of a Muslim community today. Against this, there are strong traditions that the Prophet himself adhered to decisions arrived at through *shūrā*, for example in the matter of going into battle at Uhud, and this has implications, *a fortiori*, for the leaders who follow. Q4:58, 59 have sometimes been taken to mean that the community appoints those who have authority over them. Whatever the meaning of these, in the earliest period it is true that the Caliph was elected, in one way or another, and that even when the office had become hereditary *de facto*, the fiction of election was preserved. This was particularly preserved in the continuation of the tribal custom of *baiʻa*, by which the ruler and the ruled bind themselves to one another in a solemn covenant.

---

167   Montgomery Watt, *Muhammad: Prophet and Statesman*, OUP, Oxford, 1964, pp. 93ff.

GOVERNMENT BY CONSENT

For some commentators on Islamic polity, the admittedly diverse nature of the umma, the process of *shūrā* and that of *baī'a* provide a sufficient basis for government by consent, and even the change of government through consensus. Others would go further and claim that multi-party democracy, universal franchise, including women and non-Muslims, and the rule of law can all be derived from these ideas. Yet others would acknowledge the limited range of the classical notions of consultation, allegiance and assembly, but would argue that they provide a basis for development in Islamic polity.[168] It should be noted, however, that for most Muslims, *shūrā* is not just about counting votes. It is about participating in consensus. As 'Allāma Iqbal famously said, 'in democracies, people are counted; in *shūrā*, they are weighed'.

Apart from the strictly Islamic aspects of governance, we need to note also the place of the customary in many predominantly Muslim societies. Indeed, in some such societies Islamic law itself can recognize the place of custom (*'āda*) and, especially, the way in which people relate to the State and to their communities. It can, therefore, lead to a distinguishing between 'sacred' and secular spheres, even if this is not always the case. Historically, *'ādat* law has been given a place in the Muslim areas of south-east Asia, but, more recently, there have been attempts elsewhere to use customary institutions to further government by consent, as well as change of government by consent; and these deserve further study. An obvious example is the way in which the

---

168 On all of this see the articles by Fathi Osman, Zeenat Shaukat Ali and Khalid Duran in Race and Shafer, *Religions in Dialogue*, pp. 111ff.

Loya Jirga has been used in post-Tālibān Afghanistan. A customary institution, the *jirga*, which is generally used to gather elders so that they may decide local cases and deliberate on community issues, has been widened and modified (for example, by including women) so that it can serve as a nationally representative body. This seems to have 'connected' with the Afghan people, and there is a chance that such a form of government by consent will succeed because it is rooted in the local culture. As we have seen, in lands that have an Ottoman background, any attempt to establish structures of governance must take into account the tensions between centralization and autonomy, particularly among the *millets*, throughout the Ottoman period. This must mean that in countries like Iraq where there has been a high level of regional autonomy, strong ethnic consciousness and flourishing *millets*, a unitary system of government is likely to be resisted, especially if it is known to have privileged a particular group in the past. Only a properly thought-out federal model which balances the interests of the different groups and does not leave minorities 'out in the cold' is likely to succeed. The complex situation created by recognizing a high level of autonomy for the Kurds, but not for other groups, such as the Chaldo-Assyrian Christians, the Turkoman, etc., shows the importance of the task. Not only geography, but religion, ethnicity and other factors need to be taken into account if a federal solution is to succeed.

In situations where Muslims are relatively new arrivals, as in the Western World, they are beginning to make their presence felt. They have been able to challenge at least some secularist assumptions, and they have been able to show that religious belief is so important for some people that it is a primary marker of their identity. Both public services and the commercial sector are recognizing their specific needs and making provision for them in the areas of health care, banking, housing and education. Muslims are also making a distinctively Islamic contribution to the public square in Parliament, in the media and in local government. In the coming years, such a contribution will have to be assessed and evaluated.

On the other hand, the processes of globalization are promoting individualization and choice even among Muslims, and especially the young. This is a major concern among religious leaders who fear secularization and westernization of their young people; but these processes can also, of course, lead to the adoption of extremist attitudes and/or to alienation from the mainstream of life.

How Muslims live as a minority, or in marginal situations, with other groups is important for many countries on four continents. We have been able to examine some of the historical and theological resources which Muslims can use in such circumstances; but there are legal issues as well, which we shall consider next.

6

Some Issues in Dialogue Today II: The Relationship of Religion to Law, Sharī'a, Jihād, Just War and Fundamental Freedoms

It should be said straight away that moral sense, like spiritual awareness, is universal among human beings and certainly cannot be restricted to those who are 'religious' in the conventional sense. In fact, sometimes it is people without specific religious beliefs who manifest the most acute moral sensitivities, especially in the face of great injustice or evil of some other kind. They can and do act altruistically, even sacrificially, and they may be better informed on moral issues than some religious people.

All of this is true; and yet it is organized religious traditions, on the whole, which have been responsible for the elaboration of moral codes by which men and women have, consciously or sub-consciously, ordered their lives over the millennia of history. Not only that; it is also that we often turn to religious or transcendental principles to give an account of basic human values such as the equal dignity of all, the primacy of conscience and our sense of duty.[169]

What is religiously or morally desirable may not always be appropriate for legislation. Nevertheless, the great moral

---

169   See also Nazir-Ali, 'Thinking and Acting Morally' (as note 31), pp. 207ff.

codes of humanity, whether the Laws of Manu in the Hindu *Dharma*, the Torah for Israel, or the Ten Commandments and their summary by Jesus for Christendom, have exercised formative influence in the development of law in various civilizations; and they continue to be influential today, for instance, in defining the scope of personal liberty or the nature of public good and how it can be harmed. In Islām, perhaps most of all, the moral code, enshrined in the Sharī'a, is related explicitly to the laws governing particular societies. The term itself means a clear path to be followed, and the implication is that this is so for both individuals and communities (Qur'ān 42:13, 45:18). There is also the recognition that other communities, especially the People of the Book, have their own Sharī'a which they should use for ordering their own affairs (5:46, 51). For Muslims, it means the totality of Allah's commandments as they relate to human life.

THE RELATIONSHIP OF SHARI'A TO SOCIETY

In his dialogue with me, the former Chief Justice of the Supreme Court in Pakistan, Dr Nasim Hasan Shah, once again emphasizes the *identification* of law with religion, since both emanate from the same source and are of equal authority as they are both aspects of divine revelation. Islām not only prescribes for religious duties but for every aspect of human activity. As I said in my reply, Islām is not essentially different from other religions in seeking to embrace the totality of human life. The question is *how* this is to be done. Should this be through the regulation of the minutest details of a person's or a community's life, or should it, rather, be in terms of principles and values derived from a religious or ethical tradition? Happily, Justice Nasim comes firmly down in favour of the latter. For him, an Islamic state is one where the polity and the laws are derived from the guidance to be found in divine revelation, *but* such a polity and such laws exist only to enable Muslims to be good Muslims and not to coerce anyone. In welcoming this position, I noted in my reply that Dr Nasim Hasan Shah had also stated clearly that in such a state the custodians of polity and the arbiters of law were not to be the 'ulemā, or religious leaders, but the elected representatives of the people. This reminds us of 'Allāma Iqbāl's vision that *ijmā'* or consensus, regarding matters of law, and *ijtihād*, the need to find new formulations of Islamic law in the light of con-temporary conditions, should vest in a legislative assembly rather than in an individual or in schools of law.[170]

Tariq Ramadan, the grandson of the Egyptian Islamist reformer Hasan Al-Banna and now a Swiss citizen, has pointed out that there can be no collectivity without law. The Sharī'a of Islam is both about the proper autonomy of the individual and the governance of the collective. Like Iqbāl, he goes back to the great Spanish jurist Imām Shātibī (d. 1194) in identifying the fundamentals of justice as being about the protection of *dīn* (religion), *nafs* (the individual), *'aql* (reasoned discourse), *māl* (property) and *nasl* (the con-tinuity of society).

Ramadan raises a number of questions about the rela-tionship of Sharī'a to society. Once again, like Iqbāl, he asks, 'Who is competent in this area?' Is it the traditional

---

170   Nasim Hasan Shah, 'Law and Religion', in *Islam and Christian–Muslim Relations* 11 (2), 243ff; M. Nazir-Ali, 'Law and Religion: A friend responds', pp. 249ff. See also Iqbāl, *The Reconstruction of Religious Thought* (as note 98), pp. 146ff.

'ulemā (scholars) and *fuqaha* (lawyers) or should it be a wider, participatory body of Muslims? What should be the priority in this context: should general principles come first or particular prescriptions? He distinguishes between different kinds of interpretation: the *literalist*, where historical structure is made of universal significance; the *reformist*, which regards the Sharī'a as adaptable but within limits; and the *rationalist*, which seeks to extract principles which can be used in the contemporary world. This last is, according to Iqbāl, exemplified by the great Muslim theologian, Shāh Walīullah of Delhi (1702–62). Walīullah held that a prophet is sent to a particular people at a definite time in their history and his prophetic activity is in terms of the context into which he is sent. Even so, if the ultimate aim of such activity is to be the mediation of eternal principles, the prophet must *both* emphasize the universality of the prophetic teaching *and* leave some room for flexibility, where other peoples and periods of history are concerned. This is particularly the case with matters like *hudūd*, or the penal legislation of Islām: as Iqbāl puts it, the prophet's purpose is to accentuate the principles needed for the common good. The application of these in a particular society at a particular time necessitates the promulgation of various rules, including penalties for crimes, etc. While the principles remain valid, the penalties 'cannot be strictly enforced in the case of future generations'.[171]

Maleiha Malik, arguing in a Western context, recognizes the distinction between the private and the public spheres, but points out that private identity, and particularly,

---

171 Iqbāl, *The Reconstruction of Religious Thought*, pp. 171f; Rahmān, *Revival and Reform in Islam* (as note 118), pp. 171ff; and M. Nazir-Ali, *The Roots of Islamic Tolerance*, Oxford Project for Peace Studies 26, 1990, p. 8.

religious identity, is not just a matter for the individual but has to do with belonging to a community. Nor does this community exist in isolation. It is, rather, in a dialogical relation with wider society. If plural societies are to be genuinely such, this situation of dialogue will have to be better recognized and resourced. Furthermore, this means that connections will have to be made between the virtues of the believer and the virtues of the citizen – there can be no sharp dichotomy between private life and public duty, even if a distinction is acknowledged. Presumably, for the Muslims this means that the Sharī'a, by which their identity has been formed, will be brought to bear on issues of public life.[172]

If Sharī'a is the totality of Allah's commands as they relate to the individual, the family and wider society, then *Fiqh* is the science which codifies and gives legal expression to these commands. It is true that the two terms have, sometimes, been used interchangeably but some Muslims are increasingly emphasizing the distinction between them: if, for instance, Sharī'a is regarded as the unchanging divine law, can *fiqh* then be seen as an expression of that law, more or less adequate, but arising out of a particular context and a specific period of history? This has immediate implications, of course, for any 'finality' which might be claimed by any of the recognized *madhāhib* or schools of *fiqh*. In fact, one of the features of many reform movements in Islām, from that of Ibn Taimiyya (who was born in 1263) to present-day modernists, has been precisely to question the so-called finality of these schools. Muhammad Iqbāl

---

172 For Tariq Ramadan and Maleiha Malik's contribution, please see Michael Ipgrave (ed.), a report of the Building Bridges Seminar in Sarajevo, 2005 to be published by Church House Publications in 2006.

identifies a number of ways in which *ijtihād* can be exercised: complete authority in the formulation of *fiqh*, authority exercised within the framework of a particular *madhab* or school, and the exercise of discretion by a jurist in matters where little precedent can be found. Iqbāl then goes on to make it clear that his agenda is about the first kind of *ijtihād*: that is, nothing less than the complete re-interpretation of the foundational principles in the light of contemporary experience and the changed conditions of modern life.[173] Other reformers of the same period, like Jamāluddīn Afghānī and Muhammad 'Abduh, also advocated radical criticism of *fiqh* and the recovery of 'essential Islām', seen in a highly idealized view of early Muslim society.[174]

Even if some of the more radical reformers have questioned the finality of the Law Schools and have argued for an *ijtihād* which would begin again from the sources of Islamic law, the Qur'ān and the *Sunna* (or practice of the Prophet and his closest companions), others have seen the possibility of working within the framework of the schools to achieve at least some of the aims of reform. Wael Hallaq is regarded as one of the leading scholars in the field of Islamic Law. He has argued that there is both continuity and change in the major schools and, indeed, it is sometimes the very processes of continuity which can bring about incremental development. He points out that the use of *taqlīd* or adherence to the foundational principles, decisions and procedures of a particular school was not necessarily a simple reproduction or mechanical application of received doctrine, as is sometimes made out by both Islamic

---

173   M. Iqbāl, *The Reconstruction of Religious Thought*, pp. 148f, 168f, etc.
174   See further Nazir-Ali, *Islam* (as note 14), pp. 102ff.

reformers and non-Muslim critics. Rather, its appeal to authority can be hermeneutically creative, almost '*ijtihādic*' (a term which Hallaq has coined). The principles which underlie the various schools of law provide the inner dynamics for the development of legal doctrine and to its application according to the requirements of time and place. According to Hallaq, the chief agents of change are not the judges (the *qādīs*), but the jurisconsults, available to the courts, known as muftīs and also academic legal authors or *musannifs*. To a limited or greater extent, they may make legal decisions in accordance with the maxim that 'the fatwā changes with the times'.[175]

PRINCIPLES OF MOVEMENT IN ISLAMIC LAW

What then can we say are the principles and procedures which provide for dynamism in the application of Sharī'a? *Qiyās*, or analogical reasoning, is, along with the Qur'ān, the *Sunna* and *Ijmā'*, one of the foundational elements of Islamic law. The conservative Imām Shāfi'ī identified it with *ijtihād* itself, and Iqbāl recounts the famous story of the appointment of Ma'ad as governor of the Yemen by the Prophet of Islam: How would he arrive at his judgements? 'I will judge matters according to the Book of God' said the appointee, and, 'If the Book of God contains nothing to guide you?' 'Then I will act on the precedents of the

---

175   W. B. Hallaq, *Authority, Continuity and Change in Islamic Law* (as note 119), pp. ixff, 86ff, 121ff, 166ff, etc.
176   Iqbāl, *The Reconstruction of Religious Thought*, p. 148.

Prophet of God.' 'What if they fail?' 'I will then exert to form my own judgement,' replied Ma'ad.[176] Such an 'exertion' to form a judgement, in the absence of direct answers in the Qur'ān and the practice of the Prophet, became the basis for the doctrine of *qiyās* or analogical reasoning. For example, although *khamr* or grape-wine is called a sign in Q16:67, its harm is described as greater than its gain in 2:219, and it is forbidden in 5:93 because of its harmful social and spiritual consequences. By *qiyās*, or analogy, this prohibition is extended to all fermented liquor and, by further analogy, to all intoxicants. Any punishment, similarly, for violating the prohibition also attaches to what is prohibited by analogy. The *Hanafī* school, however, further added the importance of *rā'y*, or personal opinion, in determining how strictly a legal position, obtained through analogical reasoning, was to be applied in a particular case. If the jurist decided not to adhere to the results of analogical reasoning at this point, it would be because, in the jurist's view, the situation did not warrant it. Such an exercise of personal opinion came to be known as *istihsān* or the 'seeking after the best meaning'.

In the *Mālikī* school, the principle of movement is that of *istislāh*. Although it is a more limiting idea than that of *istihsān* it has been, in fact, more fruitful because it requires a jurist to take into account the demands of human welfare and of the common good, as a whole, rather than just of a particular case. The idea of *maslaha*, or welfare, has become central to the work of those 'ulemā who work from a conservative point of view but are nevertheless seeking reform. The so-called 'contextualists' or 'liberals' would, perhaps, be more comfortable with the *Hanafī* school, for which Iqbāl claims a 'much greater power of adaptation than any other school'; but the *Mālikī* approach may, in fact, be more realistic in the present climate.[177]

The *Shafi'ites* have the more limited concept of *istishāb*. Here, the application of a particular law remains valid until it is certain that the situation has changed. Clearly, this is a more conservative position but it still leaves some room for the exercise of legal discretion. Even the school associated with Ibn Hanbal, which underlies the Wahhābīs, has been shown by Hallaq to have practised *takhrīj*; a system of solving legal problems with affinities to *ijtihād*.[178] The *Fiqh al-Ja'fariyya* of the Shī'a differs from the Sunnī schools in a number of respects, but I have been assured by Shī'ī 'ulemā that the dynamic between reason and revelation is also at work in their *fiqh* and how it relates to the contemporary world. When asked to provide instances of this interplay, they mention both family and penal law as areas where such interaction should be at work in, for example, modern Iran. So I have been told that it would be acceptable if the *Majlis*, or Parliament in Iran, declared monogamy to be the norm (with some exceptions) as an interpretation of Islamic teaching on marriage in the current context. Similarly, as long as the principles underlying the penal laws of Islām were upheld, the actual punishments could be according to modern conditions. How all of this works out in practice is, of course, a question which is worth asking and asking urgently. Could the custom of *mut'a* or 'temporary marriage', for example, be regarded as forbidden? Since the

---

177 On this, see the illuminating book review by Urfan Khaliq of Mashood Baderin's *International Human Rights and Islamic Law*, OUP, 2003, in the *Ecclesiastical Law Journal* 7 (35), 2004, 479ff; Iqbāl, *The Reconstruction of Religious Thought*, pp. 177ff; and Nazir-Ali, *Islam*, pp. 48ff.

178 Hallaq, *Authority, Continuity and Change in Islamic Law*, pp. 43ff.

revolution in Iran, public executions of even very young people have not ceased. How does the dynamic view of development in the relation of Islamic law to contemporary circumstances work in these matters?

RELIGIONS AND RIGHTS

Historically, both Christians and Muslims have had reservations about 'rights'-based philosophies. This is because they have seen dangers in emphasizing too much ideas about human autonomy which, for them, is necessarily limited, both with reference to God and in terms of the public good. For Christians one way of approach has been the *imago dei* argument: because human beings are made in God's image, a certain irreducible dignity is inherent in each person. This cannot be alienated and must be respected. Some Christians have seen the development of human rights awareness as a working out of the implications of such a view. Others see it more in terms of responsibility and its relationship to fundamental freedoms which are, nevertheless, placed in the context of a 'justly ordered community'.[179]

It may be that the Qur'ānic teaching of human beings as God's *khalīfa*, or representative on earth (2:30), can relate Muslims to issues of human responsibility and freedom in a

---

179   On this, see Alwyn Thomson and Caroline McAdam (eds), *A Shared Vision? Human Rights and the Church*, Centre for Contemporary Christianity in Ireland, Belfast, 2000; and Joan Lockwood O'Donovan, 'The Concept of Rights in Christian Moral Discourse', in Michael Cromartie (ed.), *A Preserving Grace: Protestants, Catholics and Natural Law*, Eerdmans, Grand Rapids, MI, 1997, pp. 143ff.

way similar to the Christian. While many Muslim countries are signatories to documents like the 1948 *Universal Declaration of Human Rights*, some have had and continue to have reservations about this and related documents. Muslims have also, sometimes with state sponsorship, produced documents on human rights themselves, which reveal the tension between Islamic views in this area and the United Nations' declarations. The *Universal Islamic Declaration of Human Rights*, produced by the Islamic Council of Europe in 1981, and the Organisation of Islamic Conference-sponsored *Declaration of Human Rights in Islam* produced in 1990, both mark an attempt to narrow the gap between the international human rights culture and Islamic tradition. As Colin Chapman has shown, however, important issues remain outstanding in relation to the role of women in society, to freedom of thought, conscience and religion, to penal codes and to questions about the justifiability of armed conflict.[180]

FREEDOM AND APOSTASY

In the area of freedom of expression, conscience and religion, particular attention has been given recently to the question of *ridda* or apostasy from Islām. The Qur'ān knows of punishments only in the hereafter (2:217, 3:86f, 16:106, etc.) but the *āhādīth* record sayings of the Prophet which seem to sanction the death penalty for apostates. All branches of *Fiqh* are unanimous that a male apostate is to be put to death if he is in possession of his faculties and has not acted under compulsion. In some schools, the same penalty

---

180   Chapman, *Islam and the West* (as note 155), pp. 113ff.

applies to women, but others prescribe imprisonment until the apostasy is abjured. Some jurists allow a period for the apostate to repent and return to the fold of Islām, others do not. Some modern Islamists, like Abū A'lā Maudūdī (d. 1979), are adamant that the death penalty for apostasy should continue. They base their view on the claim that Islām is not only a religion, but a socio-political entity, and the punishment is as much for treason as for anything else. In this connection, it is perhaps worth noting that some of the prophetic traditions in this regard note 'separation from the community' as a factor in the apostasy.

Those who advocate a more progressive position also start with Islām as a socio-political reality. According to them, the punishment mentioned in the Tradition and in the Law Schools is for sedition and rebellion and not simply for changing one's faith. The Qur'ān, as we have seen, has no punishment for apostasy in this life, and the traditions of the Prophet which have been adduced are seen either to refer to political matters, or are regarded as 'weak', relying on a single line of transmission and, perhaps, flawed in some other ways. There is a growing number of scholars of the calibre of Fazlur Rahmān, Mahmoud Ayoub, Mohamed Talbī and Abdallah Ahmed An-Na'īm, who regard the traditional law of apostasy as inapplicable in contemporary circumstances where a change of faith is not accompanied by disloyalty to the State.[181]

These scholars, and others like them, are concerned not simply to ameliorate the law of apostasy in Islām but genuinely to find room for proper freedom of expression, worship and belief. They point out that there is no compulsion in matters

---

181   Nazir-Ali, *Islam*, pp. 98, 128; Chapman, *Islam and the West*, pp. 130ff; Ahmad, *Murder in the Name of Allah* (as note 155), pp. 49ff.

of religion (Q2:256), and that the Prophet was willing to countenance co-existence even with the pagan Arabs (109:6). Given the calls by Mahmūd Taha and others for 'abrogation in reverse', that is, for a return to a purely Meccan form of Islām, it is interesting to note that the latter quote is from the Meccan period and the former from the Medinan. We have noted already the significance of the so-called 'Constitution of Medīna' for the rights of non-Muslims in an Islamic state. Q16:93 is being increasingly quoted by those who want an Islām which recognizes a plural world: 'if God so willed, he could make you all one people but he leaves in error those he pleases and he guides those whom he pleases but you will all be called to account for your actions.' Elsewhere, the Qur'ān recognizes the possibility of Jews, Christians and others faithfully following the way revealed to them (5:72).

BACK TO THE *DHIMMA*?

We have seen how the *Dhimmī* system was first modified and then abolished within the Ottoman domains. Because of colonial influence and then the rising tide of nationalism, similar developments took place in other parts of the Muslim world. The net result of all of this was, as we have noted already, that non-Muslims came to be regarded as citizens rather than subjects or strangers in most parts of the Muslim world (with the exception of the Arabian Peninsula. Here they were not allowed to live until modern times and the oil boom made their admission necessary. Even so, they remain aliens, only there on sufferance and liable to be asked to leave at short notice).

Unfortunately, however, there have been attempts to roll back history in this respect: the exclusion of non-Muslims from the general franchise, the introduction of separate electorates, legal and procedural moves to exclude them from holding office in the armed forces, the judiciary or the executive, and a host of other measures. In countries like Iran, Pakistan, certain states in Malaysia and elsewhere these have had the effect of reintroducing the *Dhimma* in all but name – even that is argued for in a number of Islamist movements. In addition, there remain vestiges of the old dispensation. There is, for example, widespread discrimination in the use of communal facilities on the grounds that non-Muslims are ritually impure. Sometimes they are allowed to live in only the least desirable parts of a village or town. They may be discriminated against in terms of access to education or health care. In a country like Pakistan, where there were Christian, Hindu, Buddhist and even Jewish civil servants, armed forces officers and senior judges, there are now fewer and fewer of them. This is partly due to 'middle-class flight' among the Christians, and also to the reluctance of those who remain to come forward; but it is also because of Islamist refusal to serve with and under non-Muslims on the grounds that the leader at work should also be the Imām at prayer.[182]

One of the main difficulties faced by non-Muslims is to erect, maintain and repair their places of worship. When I was a bishop in Pakistan, the Muslim residents of a middle-class community, who were all professionals, begged me not to build a church there. They were happy for a school to be built (they would even send their children to it). The school building could be used for Christian worship, but not a church, please. This incident alerted me to the mindset,

---

182   Nazir-Ali, *Islam*, pp. 34ff.

in this respect, of even quite moderate Muslims. Peter Riddell, similarly, recounts an interview with the Chief Minister of one of the states in Malaysia. The Roman Catholics there wanted to build a church for themselves as they had been worshipping in rather cramped quarters in the chapel of a convent. Their application for permission to build was refused on the grounds that it would create problems with the local population. The most the state authorities were prepared to allow was a nondescript hall with no external Christian symbols.[183]

THE QUESTION OF RECIPROCITY

As Riddell himself points out, all of these raise sharply the question about *reciprocity*; and here there are differing Christian as well as Muslim views. Tarek Mitrī of the World Council of Churches, for example, regards it as 'problematic', and the Islām Committee of the CEC, the Council of Churches in Europe, appears to have rejected the term in favour of reconciliation.[184] Some Church leaders, on the other hand, and notably George Carey, formerly Archbishop of Canterbury, and Cardinal Arinze, formerly President of the Vatican's Pontifical Council for Inter-Religious Dialogue, have clearly called for the 'acceptance and practice of reciprocity'. It is clear that by this they mean that the rights and facilities enjoyed, for instance, by Muslims in non-Muslim countries should be reciprocated in

---

183   Peter Riddell, *Christians and Muslims: Pressure and potential in a post 9/11 world*, Inter-Varsity Press, Leicester, 2004, pp. 179f.

184   In M. Ipgrave (ed.), *The Road Ahead: A Christian–Muslim Dialogue* (as note 138), pp. 102ff.

situations where Muslims are the majority. Leaders of Orthodox Churches have voiced similar concerns.[185]

Is it possible in such a situation of intra-Christian polemic to save the term 'reciprocity'? In both English and Arabic (*mabādala*), the term evokes images of mutuality, of give and take and of partnerships. Surely, these ought to be the basis of dialogue between people of different faiths? Could such mutual commitment and relationship then involve what Mitrī calls 'the principles of co-citizenship, equality, the rule of law and human rights'? This would mean a common commitment to uphold fundamental human freedoms as well as the responsibilities of citizenship, *wherever* the partners in dialogue, in this case Muslims and Christians, had influence or power. Such an understanding of reciprocity would be far from any kind of crude 'tit-for-tat' but it would be, at the same time, about mutual obligation, especially to see that personal and communal freedoms are respected and that all work for the common good.

Western 'rights' language emphasizes the autonomy of the individual and maximization of choice. We have seen that for people of faith, and especially Muslims, Christians and Jews, such autonomy has to be held in tension with the good of the community. Personal freedom or rights then can only be understood in relation to responsibility, whether that is towards the family, the faith community or wider society. Sometimes, tension between these competing claims can become almost unbearable. It must, however, be respected and retained if each faith is to be faithful to the wholeness of its vision rather than to just a part.

---

185   Riddell, *Christians and Muslims*, pp. 180ff.

JIHAD AND JUST WAR

The word Jihād is on everyone's lips; some want to wage it, others fear it and yet others wish to reinterpret it. So what is Jihād and what is its importance for world order in our day? Jihād may roughly be defined as the duty of Muslims to bear arms in the cause of Islām. In this sense, it is almost a sixth pillar of Islām, alongside the *Shahādah* (or profession of belief), the *Salāt* (or ritual prayer), the *Saum* (or fasting during Ramadān), the *Hajj* (or pilgrimage to Mecca) and the *Zakāt* (or giving to the poor and needy). It has traditionally been interpreted as the duty of all Muslims to wage war until all infidels have been subdued and Islām is victorious. Such a view is said to have been based on the stark division of the world into two: the *Dār ul-Islām* (the abode of Islām) and the *Dār ul-Harb* (the abode of war). Jihād, in these terms, is unfinished until the latter has been transformed into the former. However, even in the early and heady days of Islamic expansion, there were limits to such ambition. It was necessary to arrive at a *modus vivendi* with powers too great to be conquered. The treaty with the Christians of Najrān, during the lifetime of the Prophet, is an example of such accommodation. Later on, a similar pact was concluded with the Nubians by 'Abdulla b. Sa'd and, indeed, this was the basis of relations with a number of Christian states throughout the Middle Ages. In addition, therefore, to the abode of Islām and the abode of war, there was now the *Dār ul-Sulh* or the abode of peace or of covenanted agreement. Such an element in the tradition is obviously of huge value in a world where international relations are based on the premise of peaceful coexistence between coequal states. There is, however, a need for Muslim countries to give an assurance that their subscription to international, regional or bilateral treaties is permanent and not bound by traditional ideas that such agreements are, by nature, transient.

Throughout history there has been much reflection by Muslims on the idea of Jihād. The root of the word, *jahada*, means to endeavour, to strive or to exert oneself. From it also comes *ijtihād* which, we have seen, is about jurists exerting themselves afresh to discover the relevance of the Sharī'a for a particular time or place and, indeed, in a specific case. The Sūfīs, or the mystics of Islam, have for long distinguished between the *Jihād al-akbar* and the *Jihād al-asghar*. The former, or the greater Jihād, is the struggle against one's own soul and its tendency towards egoism. The latter, or the lesser Jihād, is about armed struggle in the cause of Islam. Ibn Taimiyya distinguished between the Jihād *Makki* and the *Jihād Madanī*: the former is about persuasion, as during the Prophet's mission in Mecca, while the latter is about armed conflict, as at Medīna. He gave equal weight to the two kinds. Eighteenth-, nineteenth- and twentieth-century reformers, like Shāh Walīullah of Delhi and 'Ubaidullah Sindhī, interpreted Jihād to mean a struggle against social evils which could extend to a revolution which destroyed monopolies of land and capital.[186] This is the meaning often adopted by social activists in Muslim-majority countries.

From the late eighteenth century onwards, a consensus has been developing that Jihād, in the sense of armed struggle against an enemy, is only justified if Islam is in danger. This is typified in the position taken by Sir Syed Ahmad Khān and his close associates that only defensive wars are justified in Islam. This meant that the Wahhābī-

---

186 Nazir-Ali, *Islam*, p. 117.

inspired Jihād against British rule, which had been supported by a number of 'ulemā, was not truly Islamic: the British, according to Sir Syed and friends, did not wish to destroy Islām. They were, rather, its well-wishers and wanted the Muslims in India to develop socially, politically and economically. A galaxy of scholars, including Shiblī Nau'mānī Altāf Hussein Hālī and Nazir Ahmad, supported Sir Syed's dynamic view of tradition in a number of different ways.[187]

Today, we live in a world where there are many local, regional and national conflicts. Their number is likely to grow in the immediate future. In addition, there is the threat of terrorism from a range of loosely-linked extremist organizations. The international community, as well as regional alliances, is bound to come under pressure to act for the restoration of order in such situations. It is particularly important, therefore, that the criteria for the justifiability of conflict are tolerably clear. It is here that dialogue between Christians and Muslims could be fruitful in the cause of world order. There is, of course, a strong pacifist tradition in Christianity which goes back to its earliest days. Nevertheless, in the face of injustice, oppression and aggression, Christian theologians have developed the doctrine of the Just War. This provides criteria, which I describe below, for undertaking a war or armed conflict of any kind (the *jus ad bellum*). It also requires conduct of a certain kind during conflict (*jus in bello*) and it looks forward to the *jus post bellum*; a lasting and just peace which leads to reconstruction and prosperity.

---

187   Nazir-Ali, *Islam*, pp. 108ff; *The Cambridge History of Islam* (as note 83), Vol. 2A, pp. 82ff; but see also Ye'or, *Islam and Dhimmitude* (as note 161), for a more negative assessment.

Are there sufficient points of contact between Just War theory and Jihād to result in convergence, at least, about when armed conflict might be justifiable? What about the *justice of the cause*? Can the two traditions agree about situations of such injustice and oppression (genocide, for example) that it is morally justified for the international community to act, or someone to act on its behalf? What about *proper authority*? This was and is a highly controversial matter in the context of the conflict in the Balkans, and also the war in Iraq. In Islām, Jihād has traditionally been controlled by the Imām or, at least, a Muslim sovereign. Today some scholars hold that, while Jihād is a duty for the whole Muslim community and, indeed, sometimes for the individual, the authority to kill on the battlefield, or *qitāl*, can only be provided by the state. Similarly, in the Christian tradition, proper authority has often been that of the sovereign. Must we now say that such authority has passed from national governments to the international community, or are there circumstances in which nations, or groups of nations, can protect their own interest, regional stability, or the interests of the weak who cannot defend themselves? Can we agree that armed action must be a *last resort* when all other means of resolving the conflict have failed; and can we agree that its purpose must be to free people from injustice, oppression and actual or imminent aggression?

As far as the *jus ad bellum* is concerned, there is much in each tradition about *proper proportionality*: there must be a good chance of success, and the evil caused by armed conflict must not be greater than the evil it seeks to remove. Both sides agree about the safety of non-combatants, though the detail of this would have to be settled. As for the *jus post bellum*, each side can draw on its vision of the common good so that peace can be established and reconstruction can begin in a way which is most conducive to the welfare of those who have been caught up in the conflict.[188]

As we said at the beginning, Islām and Christianity, as the two largest, and growing, faiths in the world owe it to their own adherents, as well as to the rest of humanity, to engage in urgent, regular and informed dialogue on such issues. The information revolution has made the resources of each tradition available to the other and, indeed, to the rest of the world. Will these resources be used in the promotion of further conflict or in the cause of a peaceful, just and compassionate world? Governments, international bodies and non-governmental organizations also have responsibilities in the matter. They should not only promote such dialogue, but it is in their interests to monitor it and to draw on it for their own policy-making. The costs involved in such activity are tiny compared to what needs to be spent in containing religiously-inspired conflict, whether at home or abroad.

---

188   M. Nazir-Ali, *Jihād and Just War: Two ways of thinking about conflict*, CMS Newsletter 518, June 1994. See further Richard Harries, *Christianity and War in a Nuclear Age*, Mowbray, London, 1986, pp. 63ff; James T. Johnson and George Weigel, *Just War and the Gulf War*, Ethics and Public Policy Center, Washington, DC, 1991; Bernard Häring, *The Healing Power of Peace and Non-Violence*, Paulist Press, Mahwah, NJ, 1986; T. W. Arnold, *The Preaching of Islam*, Lahore, 1961; Kenneth Cragg, *Muhammad and the Christian: A Question of Response*, Darton, Longman & Todd, London, 1984.

7

Terrorism, Poverty and World Order

Is there a link between terrorism and poverty? This is a question which is frequently asked, but which is difficult to answer in a few words. Gilles Kepel has shown how the roots of extremist Islām are to be found in the burgeoning and urbanized youth of the Middle East and North Africa. For the first time, these young people have had the benefit of an education and have been freed from the social structure of the village. They *can* imagine a different life and new roles for themselves, yet they are alienated from an elite-controlled mainstream and find themselves without opportunity – 'propping up walls', as the Algerian jibe has it. It is in such circumstances that the writings of Sayyid Qutb, Maudūdī and even Khomeini take root, and organizations like *Takfīr wa'l Hijra* and *Hizb al-Tahrīr* are born and flourish. Their leadership is overwhelmingly drawn from those who have been educated in technological disciplines and who, therefore, wish to read religious texts like 'How to do it' manuals.[189]

---

189   See further Kepel, *Jihād* (as note 121), pp. 66f, 159f; and Ruthven, *A Fury for God* (as note 122), pp. 112f.

In a somewhat different context, the Deobandī Madrassas are strung all along the Durand line in the North-Western Frontier between Pakistan and Afghanistan. The pupils of these religious schools have generally come from the urban and rural poor whose families could not, or would not, send them to other kinds of schools. These pupils (or *tālibān*) are schooled in the traditional disciplines of recitation of the Qur'ān, study of the *Sunna* (or practice of the Prophet), *Fiqh* (mostly of the Hanafī kind), traditional logic and rhetoric. In due course, they become the power-base of some of the Islamist parties. In the 1970s and 1980s the arrival of three million or more refugees from the war in Afghanistan provided these madrassas with Afghan pupils who were unwilling to continue with the traditional quietism of Deoband. It was in such ferment in South-West Asia that the movement which came to be known as the Tālibān was born. Their leadership had been formed almost wholly in the context of traditional disciplines, and they were quite unlike other Islamists, even within Afghanistan, who wished to 'Islamize modernity'. For the Tālibān, there was no possibility of Islām mixing with modernity of any kind.

The coming together of these two streams, of radical Islām and Tālibān hospitality for Al-Qā'ida (which, incidentally, means the Fundamental Rule), is one of the more remarkable aspects of recent history.[190] Ahmad Rashīd, the Pakistani political commentator, has pointed out that these madrassas are also host to large numbers of pupils from Central Asia, and that this is a significant factor in the radicalization of Islām in the countries bordering Afghanistan. We are only just beginning to see the political and strategic consequences of these movements which have arisen as a

---

190   Kepel, *Jihād*, pp. 142f.

result of religious repression, political corruption and extreme poverty.[191]

ALIENATION AND INTEGRATION IN THE WEST

In Britain, as in other parts of Europe, the pattern of migration has been of single men arriving for work. At this stage, their religious observance (as distinct from allegiance) is negligible. It is only when families start arriving and people become concerned about the spiritual nurture of the young, that mosques and religious associations, of various kinds, begin to be established. These, on the whole, represent the different traditions of Islām from where the immigrants have come. In Britain, government policy, both local and national, has emphasized the importance of particular communities rather than the need for their integration. It is said that this has led to young people feeling alienated from their wider context and vulnerable to extremist overtures. In France, on the other hand, where the dominant philosophy of *laicité* has encouraged, if not compelled, integration, this is itself alleged to have brought about alienation. 'Heads I win, tails you lose.' The fact is that, for whatever reason, a sizeable number of young Muslim males feel alienated from wider society. The causes vary and include low educational achievement, lack of job opportunities, feeling 'trapped' by the monolithic culture of their own communities, and socio-economic deprivation. Only a small proportion of these men, however, are drawn to religious extremism, though more may be involved in

---

191   A. Rashīd, *Jihād: The Rise of Militant Islam in Central Asia*, Yale University Press, New Haven, CT, 2002, pp. 212f.

moderate Islamist activity. The presence in Britain of a number of radical Islamist leaders as refugees has served as a role model for those inclined in that direction; and modern communications, especially the Internet, have opened them up to a host of organizations claiming to speak in the name of Islām.[192]

It is understood that at this time a security task has to be carried out, and that those who are involved in extremist activity need to be identified and, if necessary, dealt with in accordance with the principles of natural justice. It is time also for the security services to realize that those who are a threat in their own country and to their own people are quite likely to be a threat here also. In the past, foreign governments have been in despair that such people have been able to continue with their activities in this country, both to our detriment and to that of others. Everyone must be made safe from them. There should be respect for the law and due judicial process, but it is urgent that the activities of dangerous extremists are actively and quickly curtailed.

For many years now, I, along with others, have been arguing on the basis of educational principles that 'ministers of religion', from any faith background, should be adequately trained at a recognized institution, and should have sufficient cultural awareness and a reasonable command of English. This should be expected of all but, especially, of those who come to work in this country from elsewhere. I am glad, therefore, that the Home Office has, at last, produced some guidance in this area. In due course, this will lead to faith communities feeling more at ease in the

---

192   On the background, see Philip Lewis, *Islamic Britain: Religion, Politics and Identity among British Muslims*, I B Tauris, London, 1994.

culture, even if they have to challenge it from time to time in the name of the beliefs and values dear to them.

The Cantle Report which was produced after the 'disturbances' in certain northern towns and cities in 2001 recognizes that community preference, the provision of services, housing policy and other factors have conspired to create a situation of *de facto* segregation in many localities. The Report has argued for greater integration and has identified schools and housing policy which could be used to promote this. Encouraging greater mobility among young people in educational, social and employment contexts is certainly one way of encouraging the mutual learning and appreciation of the other which leads to the right kind of integration that is not simply assimilation by the dominant group. As the Mystical Crew of Bradford sing, 'my disadvantage is my age, it's like I'm locked up in a cage.'[193]

An immediate reaction to terrorist activity might be to further reduce the mobility of certain kinds of young people, especially Muslims and those deemed to be Muslim because of their appearance. There is anecdotal evidence that this is, indeed, happening. Such a policy could, however, be myopic. It may deal with an immediate security problem but it will also create huge problems for the future. In a world where the wealthy (including the wealthy young) are increasingly mobile, it will increase frustration to boiling point if Muslims, and especially young Muslims, feel 'corralled' for security reasons.

---

193 *Community Cohesion: A Report of the Independent Review Team*, Home Office, n.d.

THE INTERNATIONAL SITUATION

What is sauce for the goose . . . As in Britain, so elsewhere, steps have to be taken to promote greater integration. The Government of Pakistan's programme to widen the *curricula* of the madrassas so that, alongside religious knowledge, the pupils also study modern subjects and acquire skills which will assist in employment in the future, is very imaginative in its conception. Whether it can be delivered is another matter: there is a huge challenge in terms of training or re-training of teachers, providing sometimes capital-intensive equipment and monitoring its use. With its narrow fiscal base, Pakistan is, on its own, unlikely to succeed in such a venture. Foreign assistance is a significant factor, if it is forthcoming, but, in the end, the government needs to persist with the reform of the fiscal structure of the country, hard as it may seem, and vested interests there certainly are. Only then can such programmes succeed. As in other areas, so here also, good governance is the key to success.

We have an international situation, then, where there are large numbers of urbanized and semi-urbanized young people who have enough education to, at least, imagine a life different from that of their forefathers. Corruption, the concentration of wealth in the hands of the few, and the difficulty which international organizations have in reaching them have denied these young people the opportunities they deserve and have made them open to extremists' programmes. Their leaders, again, are people who may be educated technologically but have little grounding in the wider tradition and who lack access to those who wield power. It is no wonder that they turn to a particular interpretation of Islām to challenge and change the unjust order which they experience.

At the same time, there are the absolutely poor and illiterate masses who can also be recruited to a cause, as they have nothing to lose. The emergence of extremist movements is a coming together of these elements, often enabled by wealthy entrepreneurs (like Osama bin Laden), voluntary associations with a number of wealthy donors, state-sponsored programmes for the promotion of Islām, and great power politics. At different times and in particular places, each of these has played a part in the emergence of extremist movements.

Foreign policy *does* need to concentrate on choking off the money and arms supply to these organizations, and there have been some gains in this respect; but even more important is the necessity of widening exchange programmes so that they are no longer biased in favour of technology. We have seen that, at best, technology is morally neutral. Rather, these programmes should take full account of culture, history and religion, as well as science and technology, so that there is a fully-rounded appreciation of the mutuality possible between people of different cultures. In particular, we need to make sure that these programmes include not just the social and educational elite but the disenfranchized young. Bringing together 'decision-makers' for reflection and training is also very useful. Initiatives exist already for armed forces officers and legislators, but they could be extended to include civil servants and diplomats in a systematic and integrated way.

Where the absolutely poor are concerned, in addition to educational opportunity, there is an urgent task for governments, banks and voluntary agencies in establishing and operating micro-enterprise schemes among the poor. It is important for such schemes to be targeted at the very poor, rather than the relatively well-off, and, therefore, to encourage the borrowing of small sums to start modest businesses such as poultry-keeping, small-scale retail, candle-making, handicrafts, textile-goods, repair services, and so on. Secondly, they should be community-based so that the community guarantees that loans will be repaid, which enables the virtuous cycle to continue. Thirdly, they should focus on enabling women economically: not only are they reliable borrowers, but their activity often benefits the whole family. Lending to women also, of course, enhances their standing in society. Experience tells us that training in marketing their goods and the opening of local and global markets to small-scale entrepreneurs is vital if there is to be effective economic enabling of this kind. Large Western and other buyers have to be conscientized about the need to support such people, even if this is not always as cost-effective as they would like it to be.

DEALING WITH THE FLASH-POINTS

Finally, the international community, as a whole, and the great powers, in particular, need to deal with the so-called 'flash-points' which can trigger and sustain involvement in extremism. If the Israel-Palestine situation were to be resolved in a just and peaceful way, this would remove a huge plank in the strategies of extremist leaders. Similarly, as we have seen already, no Pakistani leader can completely and effectively check extremism unless the Kashmir dispute is resolved. If India and Pakistan truly want to address extremist involvement, they must move to a quick and just settlement of this long-festering sore at the heart of South Asia. Nothing should stand in the way on either side and, if it will help, international involvement should be sought.

The former Yugoslavia presents a challenge to the wider European community. In Bosnia and Kosovo, the situation remains extremely fragile and a kind of 'peace' is maintained only because of the presence of external forces. If Europe can help to build a lasting peace in the Balkans, that would be a signal that Muslims and Christians can live together. Turkey has quite a lot to do in terms of putting its house in order: ethnic and religious rights need to be recognized, there has to be respect for certain fundamental freedoms both in law and in practice, and economic development has to be more evenly spread across the country and its different communities. It is important, however, for Europe to continue to give Turkey the right signals as these will reassure the Muslims in the rest of Europe as to their place in its body politic. Military involvement in Iraq and Afghanistan has to be sensitive to wide-spread Muslim opposition to the presence of outside forces. As soon as the security situation allows, such involvement should be ended, and 'Irāqīs and Afghans encouraged to govern themselves in ways appropriate to their genius, while the international community remains alert to the need for peace, benign governance and equality for all citizens. A desire for peace with justice in some of these parts of the world would go a long way to meeting those legitimate grievances which can be distorted into extremist causes.

To answer the question with which we began, yes there *is* a link between poverty and terrorism, but it is not just cause and effect. There are other significant factors involved and these, as well as poverty, will have to be addressed if the present form of extremism is to be checked and defeated.

8

A Final Thought:
The Birth-Pangs of a New World

Kimshab jahān-i-hāmila za'īd jahān-i-javedān.
'For tonight this pregnant world gives birth to the
Eternal world'.[194]

(Rūmī)

We live in a quickly changing world where it is possible for
ideas and movements to travel quickly. This is good when
these promote prosperity, human welfare and the wellbeing
of creation as a whole. We are, however, only too aware of
the likelihood that evil may also spread in this way and that
destructive forces may destroy the goodwill and friendships
which have been built up over generations among individuals, cultures, faiths and nations.

St Paul, not unlike Rūmī, is aware of the cosmic struggle
which is taking place, and he too describes it in terms of
pain and sorrow. The result of it, though, is to be the
redeeming of this world and of ourselves (Rom. 8:22–23).
The dominant picture in the Bible is not so much the anni-
hilation of the present universe but its *transformation*

---

194 *Dīwān-i-Shams-i-Tabrīzī*, (ed. R. A. Nicholson), CUP, Cambridge,
1898, p. 142.

(e.g. Isa. 65:17, Rev. 21:1). In the biblical scheme of things, the transformation of the universe so that it fulfils the purpose for which it has been created is very closely tied up with human destiny. In fact, it is in the Resurrection of Jesus from the dead that we see the first fruits of what such transformation may be like; and we also see such transformation, painfully but really, being wrought in us (2 Cor. 5:21). There is a profound connection between God's affirmation of the created order in the Resurrection and our own participation in this process of renewal.[195] As Jesus says to his disciples in the Johannine farewell discourses: 'When a woman is in travail she has sorrow, because her hour has come; but when she is delivered of the child, she no longer remembers the anguish, for joy that a person has been born into the world. So you have sorrow now, but I will see you again and your hearts will rejoice, and no one will take your joy from you' (Jn 16:21–2). It is as we are changed, transformed into the likeness of Christ, that the universe accompanies us so that God may be all in all (1 Cor. 15:28).

We have seen that the innateness of the spiritual in us and, indeed, in the world as a whole, can be harnessed for oppression, captivity and death. Religion, as an outward and collective expression of the spiritual, can and does contribute to conflict and needless suffering, as can other fundamental aspects of the human condition. It can and does, however, also contribute to a personal sense of significance, to an appreciation of meaning in this universe, and to social structures oriented towards justice and compassion. It can provide both the basis for social stability and the means for challenging injustice within society. Most of all,

---

195   See further Oliver O'Donovan, *Resurrection and Moral Order: An Outline for Evangelical Ethics*, Inter-Varsity Press, Leicester, 1986.

it provides us with hope for the future. We can certainly contribute towards the realization of a hopeful future but, in our weakness, we are also reassured that this future is being brought about by One infinitely greater than ourselves.

We come to dialogue then with our fellow human beings as realists, knowing our capacity for wrong thinking and wrongdoing. But we also come hopefully, knowing that God is at work in his world, bringing order out of chaos, healing from suffering, and good from evil.[196] We are encouraged by the increasing willingness for women and men of faith everywhere to examine carefully the foundations of their faith. This willingness for self-criticism is often but a prelude to spiritual renewal. We pray that may be so. We are encouraged also that a number of disciplines are, once again, taking an interest in the spiritual and also in forms of organized religion. This will surely contribute to that greater wholeness of knowledge about us and our world which is so necessary for an informed and truly educated life.

We are fully aware of the urgency of the situation, and long for others, too, that they may appreciate the many facets of it. In these lectures, we have been able to touch on only some of these. Although the situation is urgent, even critical, we remain hopeful. This is not only because we know that there are many men and women striving for truth and looking for love, but also because we trust in the God who has shown us something of his purposes in the living, teaching, feeding, healing, dying and rising of Jesus. We know that this God has not left himself without witness anywhere (Acts 14:17). God is, indeed, working his purposes out. Our task is to understand what these are, in

---

196   See further Nazir-Ali, *Citizens and Exiles* (as note 6), pp. 115ff.

any given situation, and then, prayerfully, to make our own humble contribution of thought and action, of justice and love, of witness and service, towards the fulfilling of these purposes.

> His purposes will ripen fast,
> Unfolding every hour;
> The bud may have a bitter taste,
> But sweet will be the flower.

(William Cowper)

Select Bibliography

Ahmed, A. S., *Living Islam*, BBC, London, 1993.

—— *Islam Under Siege*, Polity, Cambridge, 2003.

Armstrong, K., *History of Jerusalem: One City, Three Faiths*, HarperCollins, London, 2005.

Ateek, N., *Justice and only Justice: A Palestinian Theology of Liberation*, Orbis, New York, 1989.

Bowker, J. (ed.), *The Oxford Dictionary of World Religions*, Oxford University Press, Oxford, 1997.

Brueggemann, W., *The Prophetic Imagination*, Fortress Press, Philadelphia, PA, 1978.

Chapman, Colin, *Islam and the West*, Paternoster, Carlisle, 1998.

—— *Whose Promised Land?*, Lion, Oxford, rev. edn, 2002.

—— *Whose Holy City? Jerusalem and the Israeli–Palestinian Conflict*, Lion, Oxford, 2004.

Cohn-Sherbok, D., *On Earth as it is in Heaven*, Orbis, New York, 1987.

Cragg, K., *The Arab Christian*, Mowbray, London, 1992.

Croner, Helga (ed.), *Stepping Stones to Further Jewish–Christian Relations*, Stimulus, London, 1977.

—— *More Stepping Stones to Jewish–Christian Relations*, Stimulus, London, 1985.

Davie, G., *Europe: The Exceptional Case, Parameters of Faith in the Modern World*, Darton, Longman & Todd, London, 2002.

Edwards, D., *Christian England*, Collins, London, 1988.

Gilbert, M., *Israel: A History*, William Morrow & Company, London, 1998.

Gopin, M., *Holy War, Holy Peace: How Religion Can Bring Peace to the Middle East*, Oxford University Press, New York, 1992.

Halliday, F., *Two Hours that Shook the World*, Saqi Books, London, 2002.

Holt, P. M. *et al.* (eds), *The Cambridge History of Islam*, Cambridge University Press, Cambridge, 1977.

Ipgrave, M. (ed.), *The Road Ahead: A Christian–Muslim Dialogue*, Church House Publishing, London, 2002.

—— (ed.), *Scriptures in Dialogue*, Church House Publishing, London, 2004.

Kepel, G., *Jihād: The Trail of Political Islam*, I B Tauris, London, 2003.

Lewis, P., *Islamic Britain: Religion, Politics and Identity among British Muslims*, I B Tauris, London, 1994.

Marty, M. E., *When Faiths Collide*, Blackwell, Oxford, 2005.

McManners, J. (ed.), *The Oxford Illustrated History of Christianity*, Oxford University Press, Oxford, 1990.

Petito, F. and Hatzopoulos, P. (eds), *Religion in International Relations: The Return from Exile*, Palgrave Macmillan, New York, 2003.

Rashīd, A., *Jihād: The Rise of Militant Islam in Central Asia*, Yale University Press, New Haven, CT, 2002.

Riddell, P., *Christians and Muslims: Pressure and potential in a post 9/11 World*, Inter-Varsity Press, Leicester, 2004.

Ruthven, M., *Islam: A Very Short Introduction*, Oxford University Press, Oxford, 2002.

—— *A Fury for God: The Islamic Attack on America*, Granta, London, 2002.

Silber, L. and Little, A., The *Death of Yugoslavia*, Penguin/ BBC, London, 1995.

The Cambridge History of South-East Asia, Cambridge University Press, Cambridge, (Vol. I), 1994.

The New Cambridge History of India (Series Editors: M. Ackland/ G.Johnson), Cambridge University Press, Cambridge, 1988–.

Tolan, J. V. (ed)., *Medieval Christian Perceptions of Islam*, Routledge, New York, 2000.

Ye'or, B., *The Decline of Eastern Christianity under Islam*, Associated University Presses, New Jersey, 1996.

—— *Eurabia: The Euro–Arab Axis*, Fairleigh Dickinson, Madison, 2005.

Relevant publications by the author

'Christian–Muslim Relations', *Crucible*, April–June 2003.

'Thinking and Acting Morally', *Crucible*, October–December 2002.

(with Chris Stone), *Understanding My Muslim Neighbour*, Canterbury Press, Norwich, 2002.

Shapes of the Church to Come, Kingsway, Eastbourne, 2001.

Citizens and Exiles: Christian Faith in a Plural World, SPCK, London, 1998.

The Search for Faith and the Witness of the Church (Chair of the Ecumenical Report), Church House Publishing, London, 1996.

Mission and Dialogue: Proclaiming the Gospel Afresh in Every Age, SPCK, London, 1995.

From Everywhere to Everywhere: A World View of Christian Mission, Collins, London, 1990.

The Roots of Islamic Tolerance: Origin and Development, Oxford Project for Peace Studies, 26, 1990.

Frontiers in Muslim–Christian Encounter, Regnum, Oxford, 1987.

Islam: A Christian Perspective, Paternoster Press, Exeter, 1983.

Index of Biblical and Qurānic References

Index of Biblical and Qurānic References

Index

181

Index

Index

Index

Index

Index